Declutter

Debora Robertson is an author and journalist who has written for major publications including the *Telegraph*, the *Daily Mail*, the *Times*, the *Guardian*, *Delicious* magazine, *BBC Good Food*, *Red*, *Country Living* and *Sainsbury's Magazine*. Her books and articles cover all things food, drink, garden and home related.

*We shape our dwellings and
afterwards our dwellings shape us.*
WINSTON CHURCHILL

Declutter

The get-real guide to creating calm from chaos

Debora Robertson

Illustrations by Alyana Cazalet

Kyle Books

For Bryan and Wendy ... *who taught me that*

home is about people, ...

An Hachette UK Company

www.hachette.co.uk

First published in Great Britain in 2018 by Kyle Books, an imprint of

Carmelite House

50 Victoria Embankment

London EC4Y 0DZ

www.kylebooks.co.uk

ISBN: 978 0 85783 484 3

Distributed in the US by Hachette Book Group, 1290 Avenue of the Americas,

4th and 5th Floors, New York, NY 10104

Distributed in Canada by Canadian Manda Group, 664 Annette St., Toronto, Ontario, Canada M6S 2C8

Editor: **Tara O'Sullivan**
Editorial Assistant: **Sarah Kyle**
Illustrator: **Alyana Cazalet**
Designer: **Cathy McKinnon**
Production: **Lisa Pinnell**

A Cataloguing in Publication record for this title is available from the British Library

Printed and bound in China

10 9 8 7 6 5 4 3 2 1

Contents

Introduction	*Creating calm from chaos*	6
Chapter 1	*Getting started*	14
Chapter 2	*Cooking and eating*	62
Chapter 3	*Living*	82
Chapter 4	*Working and feeling*	100
Chapter 5	*Sleeping, dressing and relaxing*	117
Chapter 6	*Bathing and laundry*	139
Chapter 7	*Around the edges*	152
Chapter 8	*Keeping it clean*	161

Creating calm from chaos

What do you want your life to look like?

A year from now, you may wish

you had started today.

KAREN LAMB

What do you want your life to look like? If you have picked up this book, I'm guessing not like it looks right now. Too much stuff and not enough space to store it? Too much time spent feeling overwhelmed, not enough calm? Weekends full of To-Do lists that never seem to get any shorter? Terrified that anyone might just drop in? Instead of nurturing you, is your home a source of stress, guilt and even shame?

You are not alone. It's the nature of modern life that new possessions flood into our homes all the time. When a T-shirt is as cheap as a sandwich, every newspaper comes with a hundredweight of supplements and the online shopping emporia never close, is it surprising that we find ourselves swamped beneath things we neither love, want nor need?

I know how you feel because I have been right where you are now. When I first moved to London after I graduated 30 years ago, I had a suitcase, a typewriter (they really did exist) and a small room on the top floor of a friend's house. Over the years, I moved to larger places, but I never seemed to have more *space*.

I have always loved decorating and furnishing my homes with a mixture of new things, family pieces that have been handed on to us, objects I've hunted down at antiques fairs and auction houses, and prizes I've lugged back from holidays abroad. I work as a food writer and often have photo shoots at my house, and this emboldened and enabled me as I picked up another bashed-up old pan, vintage tablecloth or set of plates. ('They'll come in useful,' I'd say, as much to myself as to my husband, as I loaded another boxful of treasures into the car.) And then there were the books. Thousands of them. I've always loved to read and have never met a bookshop I could walk past. Add to this that, for my job, I'm sent the latest cookbooks to review and, well, let's just say Ikea's Billy bookcase and I have become very good friends.

What I am saying to you is that I am not one of nature's minimalists. I like things. Lots of them. My house is colourful, comfortable and welcoming, which is important as no one loves a party more than me. Dinner for ten, lunch for twenty, drinks for fifty, family Easters and Christmases – bring it on. Planning menus is my yoga.

But slowly, gradually, my somewhat maximalist house started to spin out of control. Suddenly, I could see how easy it might be to slip over from collector to hoarder. All the parties I so loved throwing were blighted by the minimum half-day of clear-up I'd have to do before I got to the fun bit of setting the table and cooking the food. Stacks of books and magazines cluttered every surface, clothes bulged from wardrobes and drawers, and I couldn't use a lot of the gorgeous, vintage-y things I'd collected because they were in the cellar somewhere and, well, you just didn't want to go down there without a pith helmet and an axe.

This is when I decided I had to get a grip before I turned into one of those people you occasionally see in local papers who have been unable to leave their houses for years because their hallways are full of Christmas decorations they bought on sale and garden furniture that'll come in useful just as soon as they can excavate a path to the back door.

I began by buying more things, naturally, because a new life needs new stuff. I bought all the books that were going to tell me how to do it and all the pretty boxes that were going to give me somewhere to put it all. Like many of you, I'm sure, I was seduced by the promises of order offered by every shiny new decluttering method I could find, only to have lethargy, procrastination or sentiment chop off my good intentions at the knees.

While I admired the philosophy of Zen-like minimalism so many of these books espoused (I am looking at you, dear Marie Kondo), fundamentally they didn't really speak to me or to seem approachable for most of the people I know – people whose efforts at streamlining need to fit around normal, busy lives filled with work or school, family commitments or housemates, and a life that may not revolve around a perfectly curated knife drawer.

Many decluttering books presume you can breezily ditch a lifetime of memories and possessions between breakfast and Pilates. You are not that person. I am not that person. And that's why so many of these systems break down. After the first flurry of enthusiasm, they are incompatible with the way most of us want to live.

The truth is, when it comes to organizing and decluttering, there is no one-size-fits-all ideal. This book will help you find your own comfort level. That may be minimalist, or it may be cosier than that, but whatever it is, it's right for you, which means your new-look life will be much easier for you to maintain in the long term.

This book will help you create new habits by banishing the paralyzing philosophy of 'should' and by getting rid of guilt. It will encourage you to keep going by concentrating not on what you are losing, but on what you will gain — space, energy, freedom and peace. It will show you how to organize from the inside out, for who you really are, not for who you think you should be. Because when we get the inside right, the outside tends to fall into place. And most importantly, I hope it will demonstrate that you can live more without having more.

My get-real guide will help you create your own, tailor-made approach, one that you can refine and adapt, whatever your situation. It will help you create good habits that you can fold into the life you live right now, without waiting for some mythically minimalist future which, for most of us, is unattainable and – damn it – undesirable.

I am going to encourage you to start where you are: in your messy, complicated, imperfect life. I want to help you see off any lingering feelings of shame or embarrassment that you haven't cracked how to do this yet. You are not a slob; you are

... because they were in the cellar somewhere and, well, you just didn't want to go down there without a pith helmet and axe.

not lazy; you are not a bad person. You just have too much stuff. Relax. We are going to work through this together.

I am going to share with you the secrets I have learned about how to deal with the emotional attachments we build towards our possessions and show you how liberating it can be to let go. We really don't have to hold onto things out of sentiment or loyalty to our friends and families. In fact, the danger of filling up our lives with things is that they can create a distraction, a buffer, between the lives we have and the calm, fulfilled and creative lives we could be leading. The risk of clinging onto the past is that you end up spending less time with the people you love simply because you are so busy acquiring, caring for and juggling *stuff*.

I am going to encourage you to act now. There will never be a better moment. Whatever system you come up with, it doesn't have to be perfect. It just has to be perfect for you. My aim is to help you to create a home which is functional, liveable, clean and welcoming – somewhere you feel nurtured. Because ultimately, the goal isn't to have as few possessions as possible, it's to have just the right amount of possessions to make you content where you are, with what you've got.

I still have no desire to be a minimalist, but now my house is ordered and calm and there's nowhere in the world I would rather be. You may be a minimalist, or you might want things a little fluffier around the edges. This process is about finding the level of order that is comfortable for you. I got there by removing one bag of rubbish at a time and never beating myself up for not going quickly enough. I simply, doggedly, moved forward until my house breathed out and so did I.

You don't have to be naturally organized to be good at this. You don't need masses of time to devote to decluttering, or a hefty budget for new storage systems. You just need to start. Do it today.

You need this book if:

- you regularly buy things to replace items that you already own because you can't lay your hands on them right now
- you use shopping as recreation. You can't resist the lure of pretty packaging, or a 'bargain', or something that might come in useful one day
- you regularly lose your glasses, keys and the TV remote, or you can't find your passport, insurance documents or bank statements without turning the house upside down
- you have 35 windows open in your computer browser at any one time
- you can't see your floor for decorating magazines which are pushing the kind of chic and streamlined life that seems only to exist on another planet
- you're paying to keep possessions in storage. You can't remember what they are
- you need to factor in time to shove everything on the kitchen table into an already overstuffed cupboard before inviting people over to dinner
- you have said any of these things more than once in the past month: 'I have to go through those', 'Someone might need that', 'It's still got some wear in it', 'It might come in useful one day'
- you constantly start projects you don't finish

- your home makes you feel as if you're drowning, suffocating or swamped, rather than nurtured, calm and cheerful
- an unexpected ring on the doorbell brings you out in a cold sweat

I am going to talk you through:

- what to do when you don't feel like it (I realize that decluttering probably isn't the most exciting thing going on in your life right now, but you don't have to enjoy it; just crack on with it anyway)
- how to deal with the emotional fallout and what to do if you burst into tears (you probably will at some point, and that's fine)
- what to do when you feel overwhelmed, daunted and like a failure
- how to overcome 'fear of regret' – guess what? Almost everything is replaceable
- the importance of setting small goals – and of continuing to set small goals
- how not to allow planning your decluttering regime to turn into another form of procrastination – keep it simple and keep going.

Get the inside right.
The outside will fall into place.
ECKHART TOLLE

CHAPTER ONE

Getting started

How to unshackle yourself from your stuff

When can you start?

Soon is not as good as now.

SETH GODIN

Clutter drains you of energy, steals your time, robs you of storage space and fills up your weekends with things that need cleaning, mending or putting away. At its worst, it can induce feelings of guilt, shame and panic, which mean you'd rather welcome a hungry alligator into your home than a friend who just happens to pop by. Pretty joyless, isn't it?

In this chapter, I am going to show you how to begin to tackle the Clutter Mountain, one certain – if imperfect – step at a time. No matter how daunting the task ahead appears, everything you do, no matter how seemingly small or insignificant, will help to build towards your goal of a more peaceful, organized life. Small steps also help to build those de-junking muscles: as these new habits take hold and become second nature, they will, ultimately, make the goal of a calmer life a lot more possible.

If you've ever stayed in a beautiful hotel, think about how calm and relaxed that made you feel. If you've never had that chance, spend a minute imagining your hotel room of dreams – give it as much detail as you can. What colour is the bed cover, how does the carpet feel under your feet, what does the room smell like, what can you see from the window? Of course, that holiday feeling of relaxation comes from being in a special place, perhaps with some gorgeous person you care about, and hot and cold running room service. But it also comes from having just enough. Just enough soap in the bathroom, perfect fluffy towels warming on a rack, that one book you really want to read on the nightstand, just enough clothes in the wardrobe, and each piece something you really want to wear. This is real clean living, away from the engulfing stress of too many possessions. What if you could carry that sense of ease and lightness over from your holiday self into your real-life self? Well,

I am here to tell you that you can. And, as nothing banishes anxiety and doubt quite as swiftly as action, don't wait until you're 'ready'. Start now. This chapter will show you how.

Feelings, wo-oh-oh-oh feelings

What's holding you back? It's not just that decluttering's boring and hard. It can be both of those things, but it can also be exhilarating – fun, even. For many of us, it's not lack of time or energy that stops us getting started, it's fear. Fear of the poignant, difficult and sometimes flat-out heartbreaking emotions that divesting ourselves of our possessions can bring to the surface – all those feelings that we've kept as neatly buried as if we had piled a year's worth of newspapers on top of them. In some cases, that's quite literally what we have done.

Martha Beck, the American author and life coach, says, 'Our living spaces are basically three-dimensional portraits of our inner lives. You can't declutter your living space without decluttering your inner life and vice versa.'

So to an extent, you need to be prepared for the feelings decluttering may release in you. If things were just things, it would be easy to ditch them. Often, they come fully loaded with emotional baggage. But simply beginning brings its own dynamism, and you can take this at a pace that is comfortable for you. Focus on the sense of freedom you will enjoy when you're not chained to the past by all that stuff which you no longer love or need.

Now I am going to do something that I will rarely do again in the rest of this book. I am going to tell you to buy something. I want you to buy a special notebook, one that instantly appeals to you, one with a beautiful cover and good, smooth paper. (Ideally, not a basic old exercise book, unless you are one of those people who absolutely loved school and really does believe they were the happiest days of your life.) It needs to be small enough for you to carry about easily in a pocket or bag and sturdy enough to take a battering. This is going to be your decluttering journal. The reason you need to pick a nice one is you're going to be spending a lot of time together, making notes on your progress, your feelings, the number of bags you've taken to the charity shop or tip, and keeping a record of the rewards you plan for yourself when you are done.

I realize a notebook is something of an anachronism in these days of laptops and tablets and phones smarter than a whole planet (see Digital storage, page 112), but even if you're wedded to your keyboard or your touchscreen, hear me out for a minute. I admit that gorgeous stationery is my weakness (My name is Debora, it is six days since I bought a nice notebook, stroke that paper, go on, I know you want to), but the reason I suggest you physically journal your decluttering process, drag a pen across a page, is not just that personally I find that more powerful, but also because there is scientific evidence that your brain processes information more effectively when you handwrite it as opposed to typing it. You retain that information better. Writing down your worries and goals also helps you to clear your mind and reduces your stress levels, both of which will help you as you embark on this process.

Using your journal

Start by making a list of the reasons why you want to get rid of your clutter. Don't think about it too hard. What do you want most? It's almost impossible to create the life of your dreams if you don't know what that is and what it looks like. For most of us, peace, freedom and tranquillity in our own homes are what we want – not that lime-green salad bowl, slightly chipped on the rim, that Auntie Jean brought back from the Algarve in 1987. Don't trade your tranquillity for a chipped salad bowl.

Write the first five things that come into your head. This will help you to focus on what you're making more space for. Write your five things in the front of your book, where you'll see them often. These were my five, to give you an idea:

- Spending more time with people I love
- Enjoying my home, rather than feeling burdened by it
- Having more time to do the things I enjoy
- Becoming calmer, less hassled
- Saving money

Remember, don't think about it too hard, just scribble. And don't forget to add a list of things you might do when you're not shackled to your mess to keep you going. Your list might include a trip to the beach or walking in the hills, simply sitting in your favourite armchair lost in a book, without the nagging feeling that you should be doing something else, pottering about in the garden, exploring a market, meeting a friend for lunch, or taking a really long bath while listening to a play or some great music. In order to get there, you need to be able to visualise what *there* looks like. But it's also important that you don't put off living till you're done decluttering. Pencil some of these pleasures into your journal right now.

The surprising burden of possessions

Is *having* more important than *being*? Is *buying* more important than *doing*? Many of us crave, or think we crave, that soft pillow of abundance represented by full cupboards and wardrobes and shelves, but it can be an artificial comfort. Every new possession you bring through the door of your home is a responsibility, something new to care for, to clean, to tidy up and to put away. Make sure it's worth it. In his excellent, thought-provoking book *Stuffocation: Living More With Less*, James Wallman writes, 'The best place to find status, identity, meaning, and happiness is in experiences.' Relax into your real life; don't blunt your feelings with stuff, or trade the rich experiences life can offer you for more *things*. Less cleaning, more living.

Making a plan

I love a list. Lists are like everyday poetry to me. And they were essential as I worked on my own decluttering process. They kept me focused and stopped me faffing about.

As you embark on each new part of your home, write a list in your journal of what you would like to achieve and break it down into smaller tasks. You will probably have a master list (tackle that pile of 20 years' worth of *Horse & Hound* that's blocking out all the light) and a short-term list (do what I can do today to make enough space to have people round for tea). Assign an approximate amount of time to each task. Be as detailed as you can – this will help you to be realistic about what you can achieve in the time you have – but don't allow the list to become another form of procrastination. What is the point of the perfect, bullet-pointed, colour-coded list if, an hour later, you're still sitting there surveying room-ma-geddon?

Here is a sample list to give you some idea:

Sitting room: 30 minutes

- o   Tidy up anything that's on the floor. If the floor is covered in stuff and you're low on time or energy, just do as much as you can in ten minutes. Work quickly. Don't think about it too much. You are making progress and you can come back to it later.

- Take three decent-sized rubbish bags. Fill one with things that need to go into other rooms, one with anything you can recycle or sell, and one with rubbish, including anything that's in the wastepaper basket. Ten minutes.
- Do a quick sweep of the coffee table. Remove any dirty cups, glasses and plates. Put remote controls together. Toss any newspapers or magazines in the recycling or stack neatly if you're genuinely not finished with them (Newsflash: You're probably finished with them). Five minutes.
- Tidy up a coffee-cup zone (see page 27). Five minutes.

Decluttering around the world
Feng what now?

I am a down-to-earth person. My northern roots make me eye-rollingly sceptical of the idea that a pot plant in a certain corner wards off conflict (though they are nice, see page 96), or that keeping the loo seat down prevents riches pouring away, but one of the tenets of feng shui – that clutter is stuck energy – makes perfect sense to me. What is clutter but the physical manifestation of indecision, procrastination and not being entirely engaged in your own life? All those piles of papers, boxes of books and bags of clothes that haven't quite made it to the dry cleaner's or the charity shop are the living embodiment of putting off until tomorrow what you might as well crack on with today. Years ago, I read this passage in Karen Kingston's *Creating Sacred Space with Feng Shui* and, despite my scepticism, it has stuck with me:

Most people who have lots of clutter say they can't find the energy to clear it. They constantly feel tired. This is because everything you own is connected to you by strands of energy. When you are surrounded by clutter it is like dragging the ball and chain of the past around with you everywhere you go. No wonder you feel tired.

This was a real lightbulb moment for me. We need to unshackle ourselves from our stuff. In order to do this, we need to reset the reward synapses in our brains, so that the high we used to get from acquiring is replaced by the absolute thrill of getting rid of things. This isn't easy at first. In his book *The Compass of Pleasure: How Our Brains Make Fatty Foods, Orgasm, Exercise, Marijuana, Generosity, Vodka, Learning and Gambling Feel So Good*, David J. Linden, king of subtitles and also professor of neuroscience at Johns Hopkins University, describes the sort of addictive rush some of us get from everyday activities:

Shopping, orgasm, learning, highly caloric foods, gambling, prayer, dancing til you drop, and playing on the Internet: They all evoke neural signals that converge on a small group of interconnected brain areas called the medial fore brain pleasure circuit – it is in these tiny clumps of neurons that human pleasure is felt.

So you see, this is what we're up against: that pesky medial fore brain pleasure circuit. But you know what? It's not the boss of you.

Swedish death cleaning

I promise this is a lot less depressing than it sounds. The concept of *döstädning* (*dö* = death; *städning* = cleaning) was introduced to most of us by Swedish artist Margareta Magnusson's book *The Gentle Art of Swedish Death Cleaning*. At its heart is a kinder, mellower attitude to decluttering than we find in the Marie Kondo books – perhaps the rhythmic yoga to Kondo's gung-ho boot camp. *Döstädning* is a process. The idea is to take a proactive stab at going through your possessions before you die so you don't leave your relatives with the onerous task of sorting through your stuff when you're gone. Grief is bad enough without having to weep over a shopping list from 1972 and a heap of mothy old sweaters as well.

Of course this kind of decluttering is a final kindness you can do for the ones you love, but it's not pure altruism. Magnusson writes:

Death cleaning isn't the story of death and its slow, ungainly inevitability. But rather the story of life, your life, the good memories and the bad. The good ones you keep. The bad ones you expunge.

At the centre of this approach is the question, 'Will anyone be happier if I save this?' If your friends and family will cherish it, keep it. If it would embarrass you (cross diaries, angry letters settling scores), ditch it. And there is nothing to stop you from doing it, whatever age you are. Why hold onto things that cause you pain or embarrassment? Free yourself from them. Furthermore, if you are holding onto possessions that you would like to pass on one day – particularly if you no longer use them – why not do it now, when you can experience the pleasure they give to other people? So for me, the key question is, 'Will anyone be happier if I save this?' If you are asking the question, the answer is probably not.

Shaking the house

Most cultures have spring festivals associated with rebirth and renewal, and many of these have a traditional cleaning and decluttering element which is both spiritual and emotional. In the northern hemisphere, Christian Lent was (and still is for some, religious or not) a time of spring cleaning and freshening up. Historically, houses would be pretty sooty and dusty after a winter of fires and oil lamps, and even though most of us don't live that way any more, for me there's still something wonderfully energizing about getting the house looking its best for Easter (see my thoughts on the importance of deadlines, page 55) and filling it with flowers.

For many Orthodox Jewish people, Passover is a time to spruce the whole house up, too. The religious imperative to get every bit of chametz (leavened food) out of the house and anything it might have touched thoroughly cleaned, is now also for many a chance to really have a good general clean and sort. I live near the Orthodox Jewish community in London's Stamford Hill and our local council arranges special rubbish and recycling collections in the run-up to Passover to help people prepare their homes for the holiday.

Iranian new year, Nowruz, happens on the day of the vernal equinox, which marks the beginning of spring in the northern hemisphere. It has at its heart a wonderful tradition of *khouneh tekouni*, literally 'shake the house'. Every part of the home is smartened up and anything broken or past its best is thrown out. As part of the celebration, many people wear brand new clothes, right down to their underwear, have their hair and nails done, visit the barber's. I love this powerful, joyful idea of transformation, starting anew. There is something enormously pleasing about launching into a new season unburdened by the old. From now on, if my Iranian friends will allow me, I think I might cease calling it decluttering and start calling it shaking up the house, which sounds altogether more dynamic and a lot more fun.

Reward yourself

We need to recognize that, for most of us, decluttering is a long process, so it's essential to plan some rewards to keep yourself going. Don't put off living until you're done. And these rewards should be experiences you really enjoy, rather than things. No more shopping instead of feeling. You could:

- go and see a film, a play or some live music
- take a walk or go for a run
- go to a lecture or take a class on something you've always wanted to know more about
- read one of those books you always meant to get round to reading.
- go to a coffee shop in a different part of town and make notes in your journal, daydream or people watch
- play or watch some sport
- meet a friend for lunch or a drink
- have a haircut, a shave, a massage or a manicure, something to make you feel good
- if you're a crafty sort of person, pick up one of the projects you've started but not finished. Don't beat yourself up for having it in the cupboard for five years. Enjoy completing it
- cook a new recipe.
- meditate (honestly, try it if you haven't already, page 123)

When you are surrounded by clutter it is like dragging the ball and chain of the past around with you everywhere you go. No wonder you feel tired.

Where are your coffee-cup zones?

Every Sunday morning, as soon as I get up, I go to Columbia Road Flower Market near my house in the East End of London. And I do mean as soon as I get up. I pull a comb through my hair, brush my teeth, put on my multitude-of-sins coat (as in covers a …) and slick on a bit of lipstick in the car. This means that when I get there, the first thing I do is grab a cup of coffee from the cart in Ezra Court. I gulp this down as I chat to friends who have stalls in the courtyard, and I am usually finished by the time I head into the market proper. And so is everyone else. Some of the stallholders store the racks they roll their plants into the market on just outside the Royal Oak pub. Every week, one of these racks becomes full of empty paper cups as people finish their coffee and, for want of a bin, look for somewhere slightly less antisocial to put their rubbish than on the pavement. And every week, the paper cups fill up a different shelf. Wherever the first cup is left, an hour later there will be a hundred more.

What I am trying to say here is that we all have coffee-cup zones in our own houses – hot spots where rubbish accumulates simply because that is where rubbish accumulates. This can occur out of such deeply ingrained habit that it often becomes unconscious. Worse, it becomes invisible.

Ask yourself: where are your coffee-cup zones? One might be the pretty basket you placed on the hall table to hold the post and keys, which is now a rat's nest of takeaway flyers, discount vouchers, grotty tennis balls and odd gloves. Or the filing tray on your desk, full of papers so ancient the lower ones might well be written on papyrus. Or the chair in the bedroom that you haven't sat on for years because it's always covered in a week's worth of laundry. Chairs are often clutter magnets – it could be because their shape so closely mimics human shoulders that we can't stop ourselves from flinging our burdens onto them.

Take your decluttering journal – or your tablet, or your laptop, whatever works for you, but you know my opinion on the magical powers of pen and paper – right now and wander about your home (you can physically do this, or just imagine it if you are on a bus journey or in a boring meeting that could do with a bit of livening up), listing each coffee-cup zone. Make a plan to tackle these. You could do them all in one swoop, if you don't have many and/or you have lots of energy, or plan to do them over a few days. Write down exactly when you are going to do this. Scribbling down 'Monday, 8pm, sort out hell bowl of rubbish on dining table' makes it about a million more times likely that you will do this and that is a scientific fact. Well, perhaps not an absolute fact, but I did read about it in *Forbes*, which is a proper, grown-up business magazine for serious business people, who are all over the idea of setting goals being the first step to achieving them. So write it down.

I know what you're thinking. You're thinking: my hallway is an obstacle course, it's been three winters now since I have been able to find my good coat, I've just bought cumin (for my own cumin-inspired journey, see page 69) for the 84th time in human memory because I have no idea where the other 83 jars are and the bathroom cupboard contains 15 different bottles of shampoo just in case Big Grooming decides to stop making it – and this idiot woman wants me to sort out the letter rack?

I hear you. If you feel you have a mountain to climb, the letter rack seems a trivial place to start. But trust me, the power of cumulative small victories is what will help you win this clutter war. For relatively little effort, clearing the coffee cup zones and keeping them cleared will spur you on to bigger projects. The journey of a thousand rubbish bags begins with the first step towards the bin, recycling or charity shop. There is never a perfect moment, there is never a perfect place to start, so you might as well start here and now with an easy win.

Be the tortoise, not the hare

Banish from your mind all thoughts of sorting, tidying and cleaning marathons. It's much more important to create calm, regular, good habits. Mammoth decluttering sessions don't work in the long term because they're boring, exhausting and don't require you to address the habits that got you into a muddle in the first place. You know all those home makeover programmes where the show revisits the made-over house six months later, to find it once again drowning in junk? That's what happens when your practical self races ahead of your emotional self.

Small, incremental changes are powerful. They are what will effectively transform your life, or at least your home, in the long term. You need to work towards your own solution which requires you to be patient with and kind to yourself (while also doing the work – you can't skip that part, sorry). In this race, you are rooting for the tortoise, not the hare.

You can only run your own race. But you absolutely can get there from here.

Why is decluttering so hard?

It's difficult because it forces us to confront things – possessions, feelings, relationships, memories – that we often don't want to deal with. But you know what? There's a certain freedom that comes with telling yourself, 'I don't want to do this, I'm never going to want to do this, so instead of waiting for that perfect day*, I am just going to start today.' Acknowledge that it's hard. Give yourself a moment. Then get moving.

A 2011 study in the *Journal of Consumer Psychology* had some interesting things to say about why, when so many of us say we want to live a life less encumbered by things, for most of us it is still so hard to achieve. The objects we find most difficult to get rid of are the ones that are the most tied up with our self-worth. It is not

---

* which, I can tell you, will never come while Netflix and nice cafés with cosy reading corners exist, and the good ship Displacement Activty still bobs in the harbour at Procrastination Point.

about their monetary value – often these things are entirely worthless – it's that they are closely associated with how we feel about ourselves and how we would like the world to view us.

For many years, my weakness was books. I was absolutely the girl who walked about campus with that (unread) copy of Camus because it was important to me that people thought I was clever and worldly. Hell, I'm pretty sure I even wore a beret at some point. So as I began to declutter, it was very hard for me to get rid of books (see page 106 for Book boot camp), as they are the objects that are most tied to how I see myself. If professional success is the thing that is most important to you, the objects that will be hardest for you to throw into a skip are trophies, award certificates, any form of external appraisal of how thoroughly marvellous you are, even if it's a Grade 1 piano certificate from when you were ten. If relationships are what motivate you most, for you it will be that worn out-old sweater your first boyfriend gave you, or that boring brown scarf you've never worn but that your mum knitted for you with her poor, arthritic hands. And let's not even get started on love letters (yet).

Seize the imperfect day

So now we've established you're probably never going to be in the mood to do this, let's get started.

However much time you can give to each burst of decluttering, whether it's 20 minutes, an hour, two hours, it helps to dive in with as much energy as you can muster. To do this, a little preparation helps.

Get dressed in comfortable clothes and put on some shoes. There is an American housekeeping phenomenon called FlyLady (flylady.net), an organizing dynamo who runs a madly successful website and online self-help group for the domestically challenged. Her approach may be a little gingham-and-chintz for some of you hipsters, but one of her greatest tips is to get dressed right to the shoes. Shoes, not slippers. This makes you approach the decluttering task in a more focused way. You're more likely to keep going, less likely to slummock back onto the sofa and, an hour later, find yourself going through a long-lost heap of recipes you pulled out of *Good Housekeeping circa* 1992, haven't looked at since, but now feel are indispensable to human life.

The way I got good at this was to treat decluttering like a job, even if it was a job that took up only 30 minutes of my day at a time. This has helped me to stay on it. So I dress in practical clothes, not something that I dragged out of the bottom of the laundry basket – let's face it, it's depressing enough without, as my dad would say, looking like a bag of tripe. I wear clean, fresh clothes which are easy to move about in. I brush my hair, put on some lipstick and do what I need to do to feel invincible and up to the task. Whatever you need to do to feel that way, do it.

I find the great thing in this world is not so much where
we stand, as in what direction we are moving.
OLIVER WENDELL HOLMES

Ask yourself this...

I've heard it all. This is because I've said it all. I've been where you are, marooned in a sea of possessions and not knowing where to start, feeling overwhelmed and flustered. You embark on Operation Banish Clutter with such good intentions, but quickly the task ahead seems insurmountable. This is why writing things down in your decluttering journal and setting your timer (see page 34) really helps. Also, feel your feelings. This is something I learned in meditation (see page 123). Trust me, I am not a natural meditator. My mind races. I try my best to concentrate on my breath, the feelings in my toes, the tips of my fingers, but fairly quickly I am making shopping lists in my head, wondering if I have time to cram in an extra meeting tomorrow, working out what we can have for dinner, is it time to worm the cat, replace the batteries in the smoke alarm, why are the dogs barking? Is that a siren? Can I smell smoke? I'm sure that's smoke, did I leave the iron on? So far, so Zen. I took my busy head to a meditation class led by Linda Hall (she's online, too, see page 173) and one of the many things she taught me was that it was fine to be bad at meditation, but just do it anyway. Feel those feelings, observe yourself feeling them and let them wash over you. Let them go.

This helped me, particularly when it came to dealing with sentimental clutter. I allowed myself to feel all those feelings which tackling my mountain of stuff brought to the surface, I acknowledged them and let them go. Then I got to work.

Don't sabotage yourself

Everything we do has a pay-off. To some extent, chaos has a pay-off. We may tell ourselves it means we are creative ('Dull women have immaculate houses' and other fridge-magnet philosophy). We cling desperately to those reports that come out every year or so that say messy people are more intelligent and interesting.

*... marooned in a sea of possessions and not knowing where to start, feeling
overwhelmed and flustered.*

Get-cracking checklist

- Your decluttering journal and a pen. Quickly scribble down what you want to achieve by the end of this session.

- A simple kitchen timer. Setting it will keep you going and keep you focused. One of the reasons we become overwhelmed by our possessions – we turn around and suddenly we can no longer see the floor – is that we're easily distracted. A timer ticking away keeps you on task.

- Bin bags and labels. You want one bag for things that need to go elsewhere in your home, one for things you're going to recycle or sell, one for rubbish.

- A big glass or bottle of water. Staying hydrated will help keep your energy up. Personally, if I am planning to work for more than an hour, I make a small thermos of coffee so I can sip it as I go and not get distracted by going to the kitchen to make myself a drink and then – who knows how? – finding myself an hour later, creating a definitive list of cute cat gifs on Twitter.

- Something to listen to if you don't deal well with silence. Personally, I like country music when I'm decluttering. All those songs of lost loves, lost dogs, lost hope, make tossing out decades-old notebooks feel trivial in comparison.

- If you're working a bit of cleaning into your decluttering session, grab your low-maintenance clean-up kit (see page 166).

One of the biggest challenges we face when we attempt to drag order into our lives is our own perfidious brains. We think we want a calm and ordered existence, but underneath, subconsciously, that prospect can feel frightening. What will we do and who will we be when our domestic environment is tranquil? If we've been hiding our feelings under heaps of old clothes and putting off our heart's desire until we've tackled those boxes that have been in the loft for the past ten years, attacking that head on can shake us. What happens when we have nowhere left to hide and nothing left to hide behind? Australian home-organizing expert Peter Walsh says, 'Clutter is not just the stuff on the floor – it's anything that stands between you and the life you want to be living.' Start that process now. Banish the mental and physical clutter and embrace a better, calmer future where you will laugh at past you, who thought a sink full of dirty dishes meant you were creative.

Don't multitask

Many of us believe we can multitask when all evidence shows that attempting to do more than one thing at once means we are less efficient and accurate. There is a theory, often cited, that women are brilliant at multitasking, but I think this is just an elaborate hoax to get us to take that conference call while helping with homework, whipping up a delicious gluten-free lasagne and putting a wash on. The truth is, no one is good at multitasking. It just makes you tired.

Do what you are doing. Give yourself permission to focus, even if it's only for 15 minutes, before you move on to the next thing on your To-Do list. To give yourself a reasonable chance of success, concentrate on the task at hand and don't sabotage yourself by setting unrealistic goals. For example, this scenario: it's 9pm, there's nothing on the telly, and you decide, YES! This is the night you are going to tackle your wardrobe. You pull everything out onto the bed and then it's midnight

Procrastination top three

One thing we clutter bugs have in common is that we are brilliant at procrastinating. It is our super power. Except it's not so super, is it? These are the things I say to myself when I am mentally stuck on pause:

- **I might need this one day** – When? What for? Be specific. Is it earning its space (see page 38)?
- **Someone I really care about gave this to me** – Honour that thought, then toss the junk. If they really care for you, they won't want you to feel burdened.
- **I need to go through this properly** – When? Schedule it in your journal. Be honest. You are never going to read that copy of *The Economist* from 2015.

and all you have done is sort scarves into summer and winter piles. You want to go to bed, so you hastily dispatch all the stuff onto any available surface. For the rest of the week, you don't have time after work to scale Clothes Mountain and then it's the weekend and – surprise, surprise – it's the last thing you want to deal with. You have lived with the sinking feeling of Too Much Too Fast for several days now and you contemplate it with dread. Imagine if on that first night, you had said to yourself, 'Tonight's the night I am going to sort out those scarves' (or T-shirts, or shoes, or whatever). You would have achieved what you set out to do, gone to bed with a song in your heart at how good you are at all this stuff, and been ten times more likely to embark on another micro-project the next evening.

Getting on with it

In Marie Kondo's bazillion-selling *The Life-Changing Magic of Tidying*, she urges us to keep only that which sparks joy. While this works for many, it doesn't really work for me. If I paint it in glitter and call it Marlon, my washing machine is never going to spark joy in my heart, though it is essential to my day-to-day life. Personally, I find the absolutist approach too challenging, too lacking in acknowledgement that life is sometimes complicated and our relationships with our possessions complex. But Kondo's attitude to constantly evaluating and editing your possessions is an excellent habit to develop.

As you move about your home, keep these three categories in mind:

○ Move (somewhere else)
○ Sell/Give (away)
○ Toss (out)

Ask yourself:
○ Do I love it?
○ Do I need it?
○ Do I use it?

As you sift through your possessions, try to think: Does it lift me up or bring me down? Does it make me feel good? Is it useful right now, not at some undefined point in the future? If you possibly can, try to handle things only once – putting things down 'to deal with later' is how we become overwhelmed with stuff in the first place. Later is now.

Another important question to ask yourself as you consider whether you want to hold onto something or not is, Is it earning its keep? I am not just talking about whether you use it or love it, but whether you use it or love it enough to carry on paying to keep a roof over its head. At a time of stratospherically high rents and property prices, many of us consider buying or renting larger homes (or in the case of homeowners, extending the ones we already have at huge cost) just to house a wealth of possessions which in many cases we're not that wild about. We're simply used to them being around, like the worst kind of house guests who don't make any contribution and expect you to constantly pick up after them. You may already be sitting in the house of your dreams. You just can't see it for the junk.

In order to deal with the junk situation or, more correctly, to avoid dealing with it while running through money like an excessively caffeinated Kardashian, more than a quarter of a million of us rent space in self-storage units.

My local self-storage company advertises itself with the slogan: 'Enjoy the freedom of a decluttered home. Store your excess belongings at Out of Sight Out of Mind Out of Pocket Storage.'* Its website explains how you will feel a weight off your shoulders if you simply rent a unit. You certainly will, but this is the worst sort of possession procrastination. A 7.5m² unit, for example, costs £70 a week to rent. That's more than £3,600 a year. If you're considering dumping it all in a storage unit to deal with 'later' (you know by now how I feel about 'later'), work out how much it will cost in a year and then do a quick calculation of how long it takes you to earn that money. Chances are, you could buy a brand new sofa, bread maker, complete set of Lee Child paperbacks and exercise bike for what it would cost you to keep the same things in storage for a year.

Let it go, let it go (you never loved that teapot anyway)

Once you've gathered your objects, the most important thing is to get them out. Get rid of them. Bye, been nice knowing you, don't let the door hit you on the way out. I do this on my Sunday drop-off (below). You need to build up your own routine, but don't let your bags of stuff stagnate by the front door to the point where you no longer see them or, worse, start rummaging through them and pulling things out. Don't wait until you have a sizeable haul to get it out of the house, because you're probably not going to be able to do that often enough to create this new habit of regularly going through your things and discarding what you no longer need. It's much better to take a small bag with a couple of shirts, a sweater, four DVDs and a comedy egg-timer to the charity shop every week or so, because this helps the habit become ingrained; by the end of six months, you will probably have moved on a skipful of stuff while hardly even noticing you're doing it.

My Sunday routine: fast and dirty

During the week, I gather objects – books, clothes, kitchen equipment – in strategically placed baskets in my bedroom and the hallway. Every Sunday when I go to the flower market, I drop a bag into the charity shop. Even though I have been gathering things during the week, I try to have a five-minute dash around the house for a few extra bits and pieces just before I leave. And here's the thing: I never miss them after I've dropped them off. Sometimes, I go into the shop and see pieces that once belonged to me on display and I'd quite forgotten I'd passed them on. I see these five-minute dashes not just as a good way of getting rid of more stuff, but as great practice in loosening the tight threads with which our possessions can bind us (see Feng what now?, page 20) – today that set of encyclopedias no one has looked at for ten years, next week Uncle Albert's grand piano that no one ever plays.

There is a lot to be said for handling things once and deciding their fate quickly. It is a habit which strengthens and gets easier each time you do it, a bit like press-ups (apparently – I've never knowingly done a press-up).

Don't make your junk someone else's problem

Throughout this book, I encourage you to divide your possessions into three groups: move; give/sell; toss. People often have a firm grip on the first two, though they can be reluctant at first to embrace the second. It's the third category where the waters can become muddied. We all have possessions that, though we don't want them any more, seem too good for the skip. The obvious thing to do is to pass them on to the charity shop, though sometimes when we're being monsters, we use charity shops as vehicles to pass our procrastination along. One of my friends works in a local one. To listen to him, you need a fairly strong stomach to contemplate the list of garbage that flows through their doors along with the good stuff. Not only do they not want your ripped sweaters, dirty underwear, stained sheets and ratty old T-shirts but, worse, they have to pay for them to be taken away. For everyone's sake, make sure what you drop off is in good nick and entirely sell-able.

Are you really going to sell it?

Another temptation is to save things from your clear-out because you think you can sell them on eBay or at a car boot sale. Of course you can do both of these things, but set yourself a deadline. Don't let it become another form of procrastination. Selling on eBay is worth it if your items have real, commercial value and you have the time and energy to photograph and list them, then package them up and send them off. If your things really are worth something but you don't have the time, there are selling services such as auctionfairies.co.uk (UK) or i-soldit.com (US) that will do all the work for you for a percentage of the sale price. Boot sales are a near-addictive hobby for some, but they require quite a lot of work for what is sometimes meagre financial reward. If planning eBay sales and boot-sale weekends for an unspecified date in the future is keeping your house silted up with stuff, consider if all of these things really have the capacity to pay their emotional and physical rent. Space is money (see page 38), remember. Sometimes it's best just to rid yourself of these possessions and get on with living your free, fabulous and uncluttered life.

Stop shopping

I recognize you need to eat, so I'm not talking about grocery shopping here (though I have opinions on that, as you might have guessed, see page 74).

The easiest way to begin scaling Junk Mountain is to refuse to let any more clutter come in the door. If you have created a life for yourself where shopping is recreation, this might be tough. You need to reset the reward synapses in your brain so that the high you used to get from acquiring new things is replaced by the thrill you get from disposing of objects you no longer love or need.

When you are considering a new purchase, ask yourself what it will replace ('one in, one out' is a good ambition; for most of us, 'one in, five out' would be even better). And most importantly, ask yourself where it will live. Be specific. Blithely telling yourself you'll find a corner for it is no good. Think about how overburdened you feel right now – which is presumably why you are holding this book in your hands – and ask yourself why you would add to that feeling with more things, just because …

If possible, when considering a new purchase, make yourself wait for 24 hours. The chances are, if you do you will have forgotten about it by then. Also, and I am very strict on this, no online shopping in the small hours! It's a little like eating

The easiest way to begin scaling Junk Mountain ...

broken biscuits and thinking the calories don't count. Skimming eBay and Etsy or watching QVC at 3am when you can't sleep is exactly the moment you're vulnerable to purchasing that flamingo lamp or faux-fur lime-green coat or revolutionary cleaning system that's going to solve all your problems. You know, those WWIT (What Was I Thinking?) items that six months from now you will be spending your precious weekend leisure time dragging to the charity shop. Don't let them in the door.

We buy the things we think will give us the life we want or the life we think we want. But then we never did read that Will Self novel, or needlepoint that pillow, or lift those weights, or unfurl that yoga mat. Don't buy it. Get rid of it. Start to live your own, authentic life and make way for peace and joy. Stop tripping up over your pretend life – literally, if it's the fifth time you've tripped over that dusty tennis racket in the hall this week, or metaphorically.

Don't fill yourself up with things – there will never be enough things. Be more and live more with less.

Procrastination makes easy things hard,
hard things harder.
MASON COOLEY

Born this way

If you're living in chaos, it's very tempting to think that other people hold some sort of secret. They grew up in perfect homes where wash day was Monday, ironing day was Tuesday, dusting and vacuuming were done on Wednesday, grocery shopping on Thursday, beatification on Friday and so on; they absorbed the talent to create and run a well-ordered home by osmosis. Well, yes, to an extent some people did grow up in Doris Day movies.

But most of us didn't. I didn't. When I was growing up, my mother was teaching full time, studying for her Master's degree, getting up at 5am to write novels, raising my brother and me, and trying to wrestle a big old house into some semblance of habitability and comfort, while ensuring none of us starved or got scurvy. My father was a classic '70s dad: he took out the rubbish, cut the lawns and undertook the odd bit of DIY. He 'helped' around the house, but didn't shoulder the burden of domestic responsibility. We muddled through somehow, things sort of got done and we always had help in the house. My mother used to say, 'If I earn £10 I'll pay someone £9 to clean up after us.' She was joking – sort of – but it's important to know when to call in the cavalry if you can, and there is no shame at all in that (see When to get help, page 54).

What I am saying here is I didn't grow up knowing how to do this. Perhaps because my childhood wasn't a model of sparkling domestic efficiency, I became a little obsessed with the whole idea of a streamlined, well-organized home life. I cook, I sew, I garden, I clean and I organize like some sort of Feminist Housekeeper Barbie. Paging Doctor Freud.

If I can teach myself how to do this, you can too. I am sure in your life you have got to grips with far more difficult things than how to keep a managing eye on household clutter. Perhaps you've mastered a foreign language, taught yourself how to code, learned how to drive? These are all skills that seem daunting at first, but break them down into their component parts, tackle a little bit at a time in regular, short bursts and suddenly you're doing it. You're speaking Spanish! Programming! Driving! Not living in squalor!

If you grew up in an especially chaotic or emotionally challenging household, it can lead to added anxiety when it comes to organizing yourself and your home. If doing chores and tidying up were used as punishment in a particularly severe way, or led to regular clashes, this can also leave its mark on you as an adult.

But you are not your family. You can make your own way. Try to stay focused on the present, and your intention to do what you can to make your home calmer, clearer and better today.

If you grew up poor, this can be particularly difficult, as the 'just in case' mantra may be seared into your brain in the most powerful way. My grandmother survived two world wars and raised four children with few resources other than her formidable emotional strength. She saved bits of string, butter wrappers, ends of wool, scraps of fabric and all manner of things, 'just in case'. But here's the kicker: as you work through your home, methodically removing things you no longer have use for, something miraculous happens. Your brain resets itself so that you begin to trust that your life will provide you with what you need. You shrug off the desire to hold onto this junk as a talisman against want.

I was struck most powerfully a few weeks ago when I read this post on Facebook from my friend Jack Monroe, the cookbook author and anti-poverty campaigner. Jack wrote:

About six weeks ago I finally came to terms with the fact that I have a hoarding problem and I started to clear it out. Since New Year I have been tornadoing through my house, room by room, every week, and sorting into 'charity, recycle, gift, bin'. I began setting my alarm for 6am every Wednesday and would literally race against the rubbish truck, seeing how many bags I could scoop up in a Supermarket Sweep style dash around the house. I put out my 250th bag this morning and although my house is lighter, brighter, calmer, airier and more beautiful than anywhere I have ever lived, I am still on a mission. I recognize that living in poverty and selling everything I owned had made me fearful of loss and overly attached to every jam jar, every single sock, every piece of crap someone else had put outside their house for free. I recalled clearing out my late grandfather's guest houses with my dad when he died and the sheer scale of sorting through all the absolute shit he hoarded (eleven Belfast sinks in a pile was a particularly memorable moment) and I realize I am finally feeling stable and secure enough to start properly planning for the future, rather than clinging wild-eyed, minute-by-minute, to the now.

I found that sense of moving from panic and fear to calmness and trust in the future quite moving. It's what we all want for ourselves and it's within all of our grasps, even if we have to race the rubbish truck in our pyjamas to achieve it.

Is your home skinny fat?

In 2015 (because we don't have enough to worry about), *Time* magazine ran a feature about the phenomenon that is 'skinny fat'. To be more specific, people who appear to be a normal weight, with BMIs within a healthy range, but who are metabolically obese. They look fit, but poor diet and lack of exercise mean that their skinny frames conceal high blood pressure, elevated blood sugars, low muscle mass and vitamin deficiencies – they are, in fact, skinny fat.

I think this piece stuck in my mind because I read it at the time I began to declutter my own house and that sense of what lies beneath resonated with me. I

*It's what we all want for ourselves and it's within all of our grasps, even if
we have to race the rubbish truck in our pyjamas to achieve it.*

love my house. I love welcoming my friends and I love nothing more than planning
a party (see page 55), putting together menus and pulling out all the stops. But
lurking in the back of my mind somewhere, whenever I opened the front door
and invited everyone in, was that all was not what it seemed. In order for me to
pull off this seemingly effortless show, every cupboard and drawer, every alcove,
nook and cranny concealed a mass of stuff. Though my house looked ordered, it
was, in fact, skinny fat. Just because the floor wasn't covered in junk or the sink full

of dirty dishes, didn't mean I hadn't wasted days of my life trying to unearth the tablecloth with pea pods on it, my summer coat, that novel I'd only half finished, the cat's travel case and the toner cartridges for the printer. I carried with me a low-grade anxiety about what would happen if someone leaned against the linen press with just the wrong degree of pressure, thus releasing an avalanche of unwanted Christmas presents (probably from them), old magazines I was going to get to one day, and that stack of paper plates I'd bought on sale, 'just in case'.

If your home is skinny fat, it's easy to think, Oh well, I'm not living in squalor, I'll get to it sometime. Because your junk habit may not seem on the surface to be as acute as some – you're not literally tripping over your possessions – it allows you to procrastinate longer. On the surface it doesn't seem so bad, but underneath, your surfeit of possessions is still sapping your energy and robbing you of the calm, spontaneous life you deserve. I mean, you're entirely worthy of a life where you can have your friends round without the fear that they might be taken out by an inadequately concealed cricket bat or low-flying saucepan lid. Get to it. Put your home on a diet. Start sorting one drawer and cupboard at a time, so your home begins to feel as good as it looks.

When it's not just you

There was a young couple who lived in a shoe, with so many back copies of *Time Out* they didn't know what to do.

Well, not so much a shoe as a flat, which then became two flats as they had to buy the one upstairs, too, simply to contain all the copies of *Time Out*, old clothes, books, papers, family junk and all manner of energy-draining flotsam they found it impossible to discard.

This couple, let's call them Fred and Wilma, were close friends of my husband's and mine when we were first married. Both were great people, fun, hospitable, always up for an adventure. Inevitably though, one of them would take you to one side to talk about The Stuff. The other one's Stuff, of course, which was gradually engulfing their home and getting in the way of the fun, the hospitality, the adventures, and generally sucking all of the joy out of their lives.

One afternoon, I offered to go over and help Wilma at least get a toehold on Clutter Mountain. I'm a great believer in starting. Once you start, it brings its own energy with it, right? So off I trotted, with my rubber gloves and bin bags. But first, a cup of tea. We found two cups, washed them out, located the teapot under a heap of clean laundry, pushed enough unopened mail and old exhibition catalogues out of the way to make room on the table for a plate of biscuits and, well, an hour later we were still there. Possibly two hours later. By then, I knew all about why Fred wouldn't let her get rid of a single ancient copy of *Time Out* (is there anything more useless than a five-year-old listings magazine?), any of the old textbooks he hadn't glanced at since university, even his old jackets which no longer fit. Annoying. I get it. But – I was treading very carefully at this point because, as we've already established, stuff is never just stuff – there was nothing stopping us making a stab at thinning down some of her own things, was there? I looked around the room at the heaps of clothes on every chair, some with their tags still on, the bags of fabric that would never see a sewing machine, the stacked-up packing boxes in the corner containing goodness knows what.

'Why should I? If I tidy up, he'll just fill the space with more of his things.'

We were at Stand Off at the Rubbish Corral. Neither one of them wanted to blink first.

If you are in this kind of situation, with a partner or your kids or a flatmate (see Sharing isn't always caring, page 53), I am going to urge you to blink first, to move first. You've got absolutely nothing to lose. You are reading this book because the way you are living right now isn't making you happy. In an ideal world, you will get everyone on board and you can do this together, each one of you taking responsibility for your own things and, possibly, for different parts of your home. Some people even make it into a sort of challenge, seeing who can divest themselves of their rubbish the fastest and the most effectively.

And then there's the rest of us. In most shared living situations, each person has a different tolerance for (you say) clutter and (I say) treasured possessions. You have to find your way through the middle somehow. In her excellent book, *Unf*ck Your Habitat: You're Better Than Your Mess*, Rachel Hoffman makes a very strong point that we are often inclined to let men off the hook too quickly, to make allowances, to argue they just don't see the clutter or the crumbs or the grubby floor, and we need to stop doing this. She is right, of course. Each person in a household should shoulder their portion of responsibility, but when I look around me it's mostly my female friends who feel the heaviest domestic burden because we are schooled, socialized, to view our homes as an extension of ourselves in a way that men usually aren't. We are more likely to feel embarrassment, even shame, if our living conditions are less than perfect. So for these totally understandable (if entirely annoying) reasons, it's often the woman in the household who will blink first and grab the bin bags. But don't be sidetracked by the fact that it's annoying. Do it anyway. Don't wait for conditions to be perfect.

We were at Stand-off at the Rubbish Corral. Neither one
of them wanted to blink first.

Domestic harmony and the decluttered home

- Don't throw out someone else's possessions without their permission unless they're an actual health hazard. Discarding other people's things can destroy the trust that exists between you. Though it might result in short-term gains, it can make future progress more difficult.

- Lead by example. Purge your own stuff first. As they see you enjoying your organized wardrobe, tidy desk and ability to leave the house on holiday without turning the whole place upside down to find your passport, they may be more inclined to make streamlining changes in their own lives.

- Make it easier for people to make less mess. As a bare minimum, ensure there are shoe racks in the hall, hooks on the back of doors, wastepaper baskets by every desk and laundry baskets in every bedroom as well as the bathroom.

- Don't be the dishwasher diva. As my mum always says, good enough is good enough. They may not load the dishwasher exactly as you would, or fold the laundry or make the bed in just the right way. Shrug it off, celebrate the effort and move on.

- Mind your language. Try not to blame and shame. It never works as a motivational tactic – I learned this at puppy classes. And really listen when your partner is explaining why they find it difficult to offload certain things. Just because it's not important to you, doesn't mean it isn't important to them. Sometimes, though, the very process of getting them to explain why they simply must hang onto their 'lucky' Paul Smith suit, even though it doesn't fit any more, because it's what they were wearing when they got their dream job back in 1989, is enough to make them understand why it's possibly time to move it along.

- Discuss how you would like your home to work and look. Try to find some common ground. If all else fails, create zones where you can both express yourselves. Try to agree that while the common areas need to function in an ordered way, you won't touch the room or corner where they keep their fly-tying kit, '70s vinyl or hand loom. Sometimes it is necessary to divide in order to conquer.

Sharing isn't always caring

When you are sharing your home with a flatmate (or flatmates) rather than a partner and/or children, things are a little different. Dealing with flatmates – and your own teenagers who behave like flatmates – brings its own set of challenges.

- As before, start by setting an example and just getting on with it yourself. Sometimes that's enough to get others on board. When they see how much more smoothly your life is running, they're more likely to be encouraged to make changes.

- Don't be a martyr. No one was ever converted to the cause by the passive-aggressive triathlon of tutting, sighing and sulking.
- Use your words. Talk it through, explain what you're doing and why. Be grateful if they get it and express your delight if they modify their behaviour even the slightest bit. This is much more effective than being cross at slip-ups, however tempting it is sometimes to lose your temper. Praise is the balm.
- Ultimately, you're doing this for yourself. It may genuinely not bother the other person to live in a mess, in which case you are going to have to pick your battles. Try to negotiate clear and reasonably clean shared areas, and close your eyes to the chaos that may exist in their own room/s. Let it go.
- If you can afford it, consider getting a cleaner (see below), so then at least the basic cleaning is being done and you're not shouldering all the burden.
- Sometimes you have to declutter the expectations you have of others and focus on your own life.

When to get help

You can't always do this on your own. If you're working full time, have family responsibilities or perhaps live with physical or mental disabilities which mean that it's sometimes all too overwhelming, you might need some cleaning help to reinforce your efforts. If you've got the funds to do this, I always think it's worth it. You can spend your time decluttering, or recovering from decluttering, while you pay someone else to clean – either on a regular basis or a couple of times a year, to give the place a good bottoming, as my northern grandmother would have said.

If you're finding it difficult to separate yourself from your stuff, you might benefit from the assistance of a professional declutterer. In the UK, the Association of Professional Declutterers and Organizers (APDO – apdo.co.uk) has listings of qualified people all over the country who will declutter your whole house or just part of it (in the US, try the National Association of Productivity and Organizing Professionals – napo.net). It might be just the thing to get you started or to keep you going.

If you feel your problem is deeper than that and the decluttering process is bringing to the surface emotions that are just too difficult for you to handle on your own, or you're a hoarder rather than just someone who lives with too much clutter, then seeking a suitably qualified therapist is a really excellent idea. Help for Hoarders (helpforhoarders.co.uk), a website set up by television presenter Jasmine Harman, after she attempted to help her own mother deal with chronic hoarding problems, is a good place to start. It has links to resources that might help and an active online community that offers support. Please do it now. Take this first small step. Don't live with the debilitating shame of it any longer – you honestly deserve so much more.

The power of a party

Sometimes, we all need a deadline. Planning a party can give you – and other people in your household – just the motivation you need to tackle some of the decluttering you've been putting off. Write it in the calendar, send out the invitations, then set aside time to clear out some of your junk in just the same way as you might pencil in time for shopping and cooking.

Ditching the big stuff

Many larger charities such as the British Heart Foundation, Sue Ryder and Emmaus (UK), and the Salvation Army and Furniture Banks (US) will accept bigger items, such as furniture and white goods, and many of them will collect from your house. Everything should be in good condition (please don't pass on your procrastination in the form of tatty stuff, see page 40) and upholstered items must have a fire-retardant label. There are safety restrictions on what they can accept, which usually rules out things such as cot mattresses, electric blankets, children's car seats and petrol- or diesel-fuelled gardening equipment, but they'll let you know what they can take.

You could also download the free goneforgood.org.uk app, which allows you to take a picture of whatever it is you'd like to get rid of, write a short description of it and then nominate a charity you would like to benefit from its sale. They will get in touch with you to arrange collection. And then, of course, there's freecycle.org, which I have used with some success, though I have also had the utter joy of people asking if I can deliver or making all kinds of unrealistic demands for something they're essentially getting for free.

The 30-day declutter challenge

This is something I first read about on theminimalists.com website, which I began to look at (as well as listening to their podcasts) at times when my own decluttering mojo was low. Sometimes, it would provide me with just the motivation I needed to get back on track.

I love this challenge because it breaks you in slowly and then builds on its own momentum. The idea is that on the first day you find one thing to discard, the second day two things, the third day three, and so on until the end of the 30-day period, when taaa daaa! you've somehow shifted 465 (*four hundred and sixty-five!*) objects from your home almost without noticing it. Admittedly, towards the end it becomes more challenging, but by then I've usually got the bit between my teeth and I get quite excited about what I can chuck out next. If you're really a competitive sort, try playing along with your partner or a housemate, or posting what you've ditched on Twitter or Instagram each day with a #30daydeclutter hashtag, if you'd like a little company and support while you're scaling Clutter Mountain.

When I first started sorting through my own possessions, I would often run a 30-day challenge alongside the major decluttering, like a little side gig separate from the main project (belt and braces). I would sometimes do two concurrently, one for the kitchen, one for another part of the house. And I would also occasionally run 30-day challenges consecutively, which makes it sound a bit too much like a prison sentence for comfort. But hey, it's possibly the easiest of all the decluttering schemes to approach and it really works.

TIP

To make 30-day challenges easier, I hang one of the hundreds of free tote bags I've been given over the years over the door handle of the room I'm working on and put my decluttered objects into that as I go along. When the 30 days is up, I just ditch anything that's obviously rubbish and take the good stuff to the charity shop in the free tote. I'm about 50 totes down now.

These foolish (inherited) things

When I began my own personal exercise in decluttering which later turned into this book, I wrote a feature for *Country Life* magazine about how to declutter your stately home (not that I live in a stately home, but it seemed like a fun idea and, in fact, those who do live in really large houses deal with similar dilemmas to the rest of us, albeit on a bigger scale). I spoke to brilliant decluttering expert and former presenter of *How Clean Is Your House?* and *Storage Hoarders*, Aggie MacKenzie, about the particularly vexed subject of inherited items. It's all very well chucking a worn-out chest of drawers from Ikea into a skip, another thing entirely if the lovely yet unloved object has been in your family for generations. With admirable pragmatism, Aggie suggested offering such a piece of furniture around your family to see if anyone else might like it. Then not only do you look generous, but if no one else wants it, you can dispatch it to the saleroom without a second glance.

For some of us, it can be dangerously simple to slip into the role of family archivist, almost without realizing it. This is fine if you are keeping truly important objects that you genuinely love – things that enhance your life today; but if you are simply stockpiling stuff because you don't know what to do with it, think hard about what you gain from holding onto it. Don't surround yourself with things that keep you stuck in the past. Move them on to people who might enjoy them. Donate them or sell them. Shrug them off and create some mental and physical space in which to live your own life, unencumbered by the past.

So now we've got all of that out of the way, are you ready to get started? We'll go room by room, one bin bag at a time. Don't worry. You can't fail.

TIPS

● Try to do one thing to help you love your home each day, something that isn't about decluttering or buying anything new. It might be hanging a picture, putting some flowers in a vase or moving a rug to a place where you can enjoy it. Nurture your house just as it is right now. It will spur you on.

● Take a picture of the room you're working on. Look at it as if you were planning to sell your home. This gives you greater objectivity and makes it easier to evaluate what might be useless, dated or just plain ugly. When you're done, take some 'after' pictures, too, and save them in case you slip back, temporarily, into your old ways. They will provide you with a helpful prompt to return the space to looking its best.

Enough is abundance for the wise.

EURIPIDES

The 10 Decluttering Commandments

Space and light and order.
Those are the things people need,
just as much as they need bread
or a place to sleep.
LE CORBUSIER

1 **Get enough rest,** eat well, stay hydrated. You don't need to do this all at once.

2 **Organize first, buy second.** There's no point splashing out on the perfect storage system if you haven't got a clear patch of floor to put it on.

3 **You don't have to be good at this.** You'll get good at it. You can't fail – whatever you do, right now, today, will be an improvement.

4 **Don't schedule too much** for the time you have at your disposal. Set realistic organizing goals, allowing leeway for tasks to take longer than you anticipated.

5 **Complete things.** Unfinished projects are draining.

6 **Good enough is good enough.** Banish the paralyzing tyranny of perfectionism. Give yourself permission to do things imperfectly. Don't set yourself up for failure by setting impossibly high standards.

7 **Acquire the habit of The Evening 15** (see page 134).

8 **For sanity's sake, store things where you use them** – you're more likely to put them back that way.

9 **Plan rewards.** Take a walk, see a film or read a book when you've completed a task – anything that will give you pleasure (apart from shopping).

10 **Keep going.** This is the most important commandment of all.

CHAPTER TWO

Cooking and eating

Mission control

The kitchen is where we deal with the
elements of the universe. It is where we come
to understand our past and ourselves.

LAURA ESQUIVEL

Believe me, if you get your kitchen right, everything else will flow from there. I know. I would say that, wouldn't I? I spend a lot of my time writing about food, so my kitchen is the centre of my universe, my mission control, where I work and play, read, write, test recipes, entertain my friends and family, hang out with my husband, reply to emails, take phone calls, nurture my plants, pet the dogs and pay homage to the cat.

It's my favourite part of the house and, as you'll probably have gathered by now, it's by no means minimalist. It's busy, happy and nurturing. Shelves are stacked with pans and plates; canisters of flour, pulses and sugar sit neatly on the counter top, right where I use them; pots of herbs sit by the sink where they're easily watered and snipped. My favourite cookbooks line the bookcase and patterned rugs soften the slate-tiled floor. It may be busy, but it's ordered, and knowing where I can lay my hands on everything creates that essential sense of calm.

You might want or need a kitchen that's more pared back, simpler than mine, and of course that's fine. If you live on soup and sandwiches, it would be foolish to give over precious space to a fish kettle and a bain marie. The key to success in this process is finding exactly what functions for you, what makes you feel in control, uplifted and happy to be there. In essence, what makes you feel at home.

For most people on this journey to create order from nerve-jangling chaos, it's a good idea to start with the kitchen. It's the room a lot of us use most. Transforming it from a source of stress and anxiety, the seat of those gnawing feelings of being overwhelmed and out of control, to somewhere we're happy to be has a double benefit. The first is that it perks us up to walk in the door and see right in front of us proof that we're able to create a space in our homes that shelters us emotionally as well as physically. The second is – importantly – it prepares us to work a similar magic on the rest of our homes, one bit, one bite, at a time.

We've already established that you are not going to attempt to do everything all at once. You are simply going to keep moving forward, learning new habits, finding your new balance, your ideal 'normal'. And as you work through this process, each achievement, each decluttered drawer, organized cupboard and neatly functioning shelf will spur you on to do more. You don't have to wait until you are 'finished' for the pay-off. There can be pleasure in the process, I promise.

Kitchen confidence: getting started

There's so much traffic through most of our kitchens, they easily get silted up with the flotsam of daily life. That pretty dish you put on the counter to hold your house keys? Can you even find those keys now under the various receipts, sticky Biros, ancient sticks of lip balm, odd buttons, business cards and Post-it notes? Nature may abhor a vacuum, but it's an absolute rank amateur when it comes to junk and any empty surface. Clutter attracts clutter (see Where are your coffee-cup zones, page 27).

At this point, be honest with yourself about how much time you have. Five minutes' focused endeavour will move you forward much more effectively than pulling everything out of a cupboard and realizing you have no time to sort it out. Don't start anything you can't realistically finish in the time you've got.

In this process, it's a good idea to put together a basket containing all the cleaning and sorting things you might need. Having everything to hand will stop you getting sidetracked. Make sure you keep your decluttering journal and a pen (see page 16) handy as you move about the kitchen to jot down your thoughts, inspirations and concerns as they occur to you. This could be anything from remembering to buy washing-up liquid or to take the rug to the cleaners to calling

Cousin Bob to see if he would like Granny's tablecloth, the one you haven't used for ten years. This will help to keep you on task.

Depending on how large your home is, you might want to make up more than one basket. My house is tall and narrow and I keep a basket on each of the three floors to make it easier to do quick sort-outs and clean-ups, even if I only have five minutes to spare. My whole approach to decluttering – to life, in fact – is to make it as easy as possible to get the job done. I try not to get in my own way by making things unnecessarily complicated.

Start on the surfaces, not only because with a kitchen timer, a rubbish bag and a willing heart, in ten minutes you will be surprised how much of a difference you can make (see Do the 15 Fling, page 66), but because it spurs you on when you can see the evidence of your labours in the shortest possible time. Let's be frank, most of us have a short attention span for this stuff. We like to be able to see where we've been.

Now, pat yourself on the back. Have a cup of tea or a glass of water to keep yourself hydrated. But don't sit down for too long – there's work to do.

What to have in your basket

- Multipurpose spray cleaner
- Dusters – I like microfibre ones
- Rubbish bags
- Rubber gloves
- A kitchen timer
- A roll of labels, so you can divide what you're throwing out from what you're donating or selling

Do the 15 Fling

Take a rubbish bag and set your kitchen timer for ten minutes. Fill it with 15 things you don't love or don't need. Don't think too hard about it – it's when you start thinking too hard you remember that the chipped vase you hate and have never used was given to you by your Aunty Mary's next-door neighbour who was nice to you once and what would she think? (She's been dead ten years. She doesn't care.) Don't, whatever you do, look back into the bag. As soon as that buzzer goes, seal the bag and put it in the outside bin.

Do this once a day. Do it in other rooms, too.

You can do the 15 Fling with possessions that are in good condition and useful, but just not for you. Your local charity shop might appreciate them. Once you've gathered them, put them straight into the boot of your car if you have one. If not, place them in the hallway and give yourself a deadline to get them out of the house.

Banish that sinking feeling

I know this sounds ridiculous when you have 8 million things to do and a very real concern that that cache of jam jars you've stashed in the cupboard might just break out, engulfing the first floor and taking out the cat or any small child in its path. But bear with me: an ordered house starts with a clean sink.

A clean sink makes it easier to do almost everything else, from cleaning to cooking, and making the endless cups of tea and coffee that you will need to keep yourself going through this decluttering process.

As soon as you've given the surfaces a quick clear, get cracking on the sink. This, along with getting dressed to the shoes, is one of the main tenets of the FlyLady philosophy (see page 30) and on this point she is absolutely right.

Maintaining a clean sink is also one of those easy things you can do to build up

... a very real concern that that cache of jam jars you've stashed in the cupboard might just break out ...

your sense of small achievements, so vital to keeping yourself going. That gloomy feeling when your sink is full of cold, dirty, scummy water and last night's pots is enough to make you want to flee screaming from the house and check into a hotel, not don the Marigolds and get started on decluttering. So begin with a clean sink. Somehow it makes everything else feel less daunting.

Fill the sink with very hot, soapy water. As you proceed around the kitchen, deposit anything grubby or otherwise not looking its best into the water. When you've finished the surface-clearing task, stack the rinsed dishes in the dishwasher if you have one, or wash them up and place them in the drainer.

You're not finished. Don't leave things in the drainer. This is just another delaying tactic, another form of procrastination, the habit we are trying to break, remember? Dry the dishes and put them away. Rinse out the sink. Flick a damp cloth over the surfaces. This means next time you come into the kitchen, you're faced with the joyous, creative possibilities of a blank slate. Future You will be so grateful – there's nothing more heart-sinking than starting your day doing yesterday's work.

Surface tension

Storing things as close as possible to where you use them will become simpler as you pare down your possessions. At the moment, it's possible that you just say a quick Hail Mary, stash stuff in any remaining patch of space and hope for the best. This often leads to buying more than you need simply because you can't find the paprika/ buckwheat flour/jar of passata/vegetable peeler.

Where possible, get things off surfaces. A clear-ish run of counter top saves time and stress when it comes to preparing dinner, supervising homework, attending to your lampshade-making hobby or whatever other uses you put your kitchen to.

Wherever you can, use the vertical rather than the horizontal. Bulletin boards keep family paperwork where you can see it, hooks by the cooker keep spatulas and spoons where you can access them easily, ditto hanging pans if the height of the ceiling allows. Adding over-the-door hangers (the kind you might put shoes in) with clear plastic pockets to larder cupboards makes it easy to store small items such as jars of herbs and spices where they are readily visible so you don't rush out and buy duplicates. I speak as one who, before I started this process myself, had a jar of cumin for every day of the week.

In your kitchen, as in other places in the house, if something never finds its place, its proper home, consider how much you really need it. It might subliminally be telling you to release it into the wild.

The cumin crisis that started it all

I'm really not joking when I say that it was a jar of cumin that started me on this decluttering journey. I was recipe testing for a cookbook that contained a lot of chillies and curries and I constantly needed cumin. I bought jars and jars of the stuff. At the end of that project, I was doing a tidy-up and I found, dotted about the cupboards and drawers, seven containers of cumin. Seven. I kept buying them because I couldn't put my hands on one when I needed it.

That same day, I bought a set of jars and some sheets of labels and decanted every single dried herb and spice in my collection into them. I put the labels on the top of the jars, cleared out a drawer and arranged them alphabetically, so every time I opened the drawer, I could see immediately what I had. When something's running low, I turn the jar so the label is the other way around – that way I know I need to add it to my shopping list. I reckon this single, spicy bit of organization saves me hours in a year. But it was about more than the cumin. The jars looked

'Cumin-inspired tranquillity.'

so pleasing when I opened that drawer, I wanted to spread my cumin-inspired tranquillity throughout the house. And that is just what I did.

It's not such a small world

Oversize appliances and gadgets gobble up space, a precious resource in most modern kitchens. It's a lot harder to keep your kitchen clean – especially in this era of open-shelved spaces – if you have too many appliances gumming up the joint.

It's time to confront the truth of who you are. When I was first married, I bought a yoghurt maker, imagining a life of some kind of housewifely perfection for which I had neither the time nor the temperament. Then I discovered that the Turkish corner shop in our road, which never seems to close, sells the most delicious yoghurt, more cheaply than I could make it myself.

The yoghurt maker still hogged the counter for a good few years after I realized that. I was reluctant to give up on that image of myself. Once I did, though – oh my – it was like that moment when you're cycling downhill and you take your feet off the pedals; that feeling of exhilaration. I tossed the yoghurt maker into a crate, then went racing around the kitchen pulling other things off the shelves – a stick blender that had long since lost its attachments, an old and unlovely coffee pot, a fancy nutmeg grater I never used, a very posh and expensive toaster that had stopped working ages ago – into the crate they went. And I have never, for one moment, missed a single one of them.

So what I am asking you is: what is your yoghurt maker? Do you really use, want, love that juicer, bread maker, spiralizer or smoothie maker? Or do they simply represent an image of yourself that you're reluctant to let go of? Take a breath. Be bold. Toss anything that's keeping you stuck in this out-of-date idea of yourself. When you've purged, you're less likely to buy more to fill in the spaces, as you will begin to love the serenity of less.

The worst 'it'll-come-in-useful' story you will ever read

If you are still struggling with getting rid of things and feeling your decluttering efforts are inadequate, I am going to tell you an encouraging story about an idiot. And that idiot is me.

Long after I'd ditched the yoghurt maker, broken toaster and the rest of that rubbish, I still had a terrible habit of hanging onto duplicates. I had two perfectly good salad spinners, two food processors and two mixers. Admittedly, some of these were things I had been sent to try out for work, but I was always reluctant to pass on the one I liked or used marginally less than the other.

I love France, and in my fantasy life I have a house there where I live for half of the year. Finally, I had to admit to myself that I was keeping some of these things because, almost subconsciously, part of me thought the duplicates would be just the thing when I finally bought my house in France. Eventually I realized that, if I could afford a house in France, I could probably afford to buy another salad spinner when the time came, and so perhaps the one that was taking up all of that cupboard space could be liberated to the charity shop along with the rest of my *folies de grandeur*.

Take a moment to think about the 'just-in-case' stories you may be telling yourself. What are you holding on to in the vague hope that it will be useful to you one day? Which items are not actually for you, but for a fantasy version of you with a different life? Write them down in your decluttering journal because, I promise you, when you put them down on paper you will be laughing all the way to the bin.

Recipes for miles and miles

Do you own more cookbooks than you're ever likely to cook from? We all do. There is also some terrifying statistic that says that even if we do cook from them, on average we make only two or three recipes from any book we have. Gather all your books together in one place if you can and then measure how much shelf space you can give them. Go through them quickly. Don't think too hard about it. Are you really ever going to make your own sushi? Wouldn't you be better releasing that copy of *100 Essential Chutney Recipes* into the grateful arms of your nearest charity shop? Keep only what you use and love right now.

If you love to cook, chances are somewhere in your home you also have a stash of recipes you've ripped out of newspapers and magazines. And I am willing to bet you've barely cooked any of them. You're probably like most of us – if you want to know what to make with that nice asparagus you just bought, you'll search for something that catches your eye online. I do save recipes I've torn out of magazines, but I am quite strict with myself. I keep them in lever-arch files with plastic wallets labelled with ingredients, courses or occasions. When I go to add some new recipes, I ditch a few I've never made and am not likely to make – recipes go out of fashion just like anything else. Of course, if you're super efficient, you can scan them in and store them digitally instead. They can be stored in the note-taking programs mentioned in Digital storage (see page 112) or, as with all these things, you can buy or subscribe to a commercial recipe-storage system – it's simply a question of comparing the costs and benefits and choosing the right one for you.

For every plastic container, a lid

No one needs a hundred recycled takeaway containers or a drawer full of empty jam jars. For a start, trying to find the lid to fit exactly the container you want to use at any given moment isn't my idea of a fun way to spend the precious hours allotted to me between now and death. Think carefully about what you really need. I can survive very happily with ten plastic containers, ranging in size from teeny to huge. You may need more or fewer, depending on your household. Try to find clear containers, so you can see at a glance what is in them – less chance of you putting them in the fridge and forgetting about them that way. (It's for this reason I am not a huge fan of just clingfilming things in bowls and dumping them in the fridge – is that whipped butter, or mayonnaise, or white sauce?) For the freezer, I like to use clear Ziplock bags. You can see what's in them and stack them one on top of the other so you get the maximum amount in the smallest space.

The declutterer's diet

If you have a tendency towards accumulating clutter in the rest of the house, there's a good chance your food cupboards are laden as if for a siege, too. There are two reasons for this. You're more likely than most to buy masses of something because it's on sale (even, in some extreme cases, if you don't particularly care for it. I call this the Costco Phenomenon). You're also more likely to derive comfort from having more than you could ever possibly need crammed away as an insurance against want, or emotional emptiness. In many cases, some of these things will be past their best long before you get to eat them. As you work through the decluttering process, you will derive as much pleasure from just enough as you once did from too much, and it's going to save you so much money and time.

Be yourself. Everyone else is taken.
OFTEN FALSELY ATTRIBUTED TO OSCAR WILDE
(but too good to leave out)

It's beginning to feel a lot like Christmas

It's a massive bore to spend 11 months of the year shuffling through Santa
Claus cookie cutters and snowman cake tins just to find a plain old baking
tray or flan tin. If you can, store Christmas baking equipment with your
Christmas decorations so they don't take up prime kitchen real estate for
the rest of the year.

Dining dilemmas

Even if you are fortunate enough to have a dining room in these days of eat-in
kitchens, it can become its own source of anxiety. Because many of us don't use our
dining rooms in the way in which they were intended, they can become slightly lost
places if we're not careful. While we're busily having our dinners on trays in front
of the telly like normal people, our dining rooms are likely to become the neglected
dumping grounds for the homeless ephemera of everyday life, from school projects
to forgotten forays into crafting, weeks' worth of unread newspapers, sports
equipment and heaps of laundry. They are the most procrastinated-upon rooms in
most homes, dusted off only for Christmas and other special occasions. Give yours a
spruce-up and bring it back into the fold.

I am absolutely passionate about not keeping things for best. Once you've sorted
through your dining-room cupboards and drawers, start using your good china, or
glasses, or cutlery every day if you don't already. What are you waiting for? Live
your best life right now – that's what this whole process is about.

But I do appreciate that this is where things can get tricky – tiringly, emotionally tricky. It's one thing to toss a chipped old plate you picked up in the supermarket. It's entirely another to ditch a chipped old plate which once belonged to your great-grandmother, or that was a wedding or birthday present. Sorting through our 'good' china, glassware, cutlery and linens can be so emotionally loaded that we put it off, promising ourselves we'll tackle it some day. And of course, 'some day' never comes.

But I am asking you – begging you – to sort through these items in the same way as you're tackling everything else in this book. Ask yourself, very quickly, barely pausing for breath:

o **Do I really need it?**

o **What would happen if I threw it away?**

o **Will I care for the person who gave this to me any less if I get rid of it? Will my memories of them be diminished in any way?**

o **Do I need so many?**

If you're asking these questions at all, I am almost sure that the answers are:

o **No**

o **Nothing**

o **No**

o **No**

If someone loves you enough to give you a beautiful gift, it's because they care about you, they want you to be happy (I call this It's-Not-About-The-Teapot-Stupid, Syndrome). You can acknowledge the lovely sentiment as you load up the boot of the car, and then get on with your beautiful, clutter-free life.

So go at it. Toss anything chipped, cracked or otherwise unlovely, ditch anything you no longer need or love, or you feel doesn't reflect how you want to live your life. You've got nothing to lose but that slightly tarnished set of fish knives and the burden of overwhelming guilt.

The shortest answer is doing.

GEORGE HERBERT

I QVC you

Whatever you do, don't watch the shopping channel, especially in the small hours of the morning when we are all of us more susceptible to the suggestion that the latest kitchen gizmo will turn us into Nigella, for only £19.99. No one needs a gadget which cuts a tomato in ten ways. You've already got one anyway. It's called a knife.

Kitchen quick fixes

If you have five minutes

○ Quickly put things that don't belong in the kitchen into a basket and set aside a further five minutes to return them to their proper homes.

○ Purge the front of the fridge door of anything out of date – old takeaway promotions, invitations for events long-since past, recipes snipped from the newspaper you're never going to make, unflattering photographs, ancient postcards.

If you have ten minutes

○ Tackle a clutter hotspot, one of your coffee-cup zones (see page 27). We all have them – that bowl, shelf or corner of the table where flyers, bills, catalogues and other 'I'll-get-to-it' guilt trippery accumulate. Get to it now. Never think of it again.

○ Clear The Drawer. You know the one. It's crammed with rubber bands too desiccated to use, single batteries of undetermined power, bits of garden string, plant labels, chopsticks in their wrappers, ketchup sachets and old dry-cleaning receipts for clothes you threw out ages ago. No one ever needs more than 10 per cent of what is in The Drawer.

○ Tea towels. The truth is, most of us have far too many. Keep the best ones and toss the rest.

○ Go through your oils and condiments. Many oils (especially nut oils) go rancid quite quickly, and condiments can lose their sparkling freshness. Chuck anything past its best.

○ Because mugs are very easy gifts when you're stumped for what to buy a person (see also: scented candles), many of us have loads of them. Chuck out any you don't like, or that are chipped and/or badly stained. Pause for a second to hear your shelves breathe out in gratitude.

◑ If you have thirty minutes

○ Clear and clean a shelf or two in your food cupboard or larder. After a while, even in the most efficient houses, food can become 'unsorted'. You're in a hurry and you or other members of the household put things back any old where; before you know it, the condensed milk is cosying up to the black-eyed peas. Take everything out, give the shelf a good wipe down. Ditch anything past its use-by date and then start putting things back by 'family' – store all pulses together, tinned tomatoes with jars of passata and so on. Put anything in split or opened bags into jars or canisters – ideally clear ones so you can see at a glance what you have. This will stop messy spills and keep food fresh longer.

○ Do the same thing with a shelf or the salad drawer in the fridge.

○ Go through the freezer. Remove any mystery item without a label (and promise yourself to label things from now on – we always think we will remember what they are, and we don't), anything noticeably freezer-burned and anything that's been in there for years. You haven't fancied eating it in all this time; it's not suddenly going to become your heart's most delicious desire.

○ Sort through your cookware. Ditch any baking sheets, or muffin or cake tins that are past their best or that you don't use. Do the same with pans and casseroles.

○ Do a 'stuff sweep' around the kitchen. All of those things – pictures, photographs, knickknacks and so on – that have been there so long you barely notice them any more. Do you really love them? Do they enhance your life in any way? Or are they just tiresomely there, drawing attention to themselves only when you have to clean them? Free yourself from them. Don't think about it too hard. If you don't love it, toss it.

Calendar

Once a week

○ Do a quick run-through of the fridge and freezer to discard any spoiled food. Check on anything flirting with its use-by date. Weave it into your menu plan in the next few days.

○ In your fridge and kitchen cupboards, move anything that needs using soon to the front of the shelves.

Once a month

○ Sort through plastic storage containers and glass jars and only keep what you need. Discard anything without a lid.

Every three to six months

- Go through china, glassware and cutlery. Discard anything that's broken. Pass on anything you no longer love.
- Pull everything out from the cupboard under the sink. Get rid of anything you no longer use, such as tatty old sponges and cloths. Move any specialized cleaning products you bought and forgot about to the front of the shelves. If you haven't used them within a couple of weeks, toss them.
- Go through your drinks and discard any opened bottles of wine or weird liqueurs – you know, the ones you bought on holiday and, miraculously, when you got home never fancied drinking again.

Once a year

- Purge your herbs and spices. Personally, I get rid of dried herbs and ground spices more than a year old, and whole spices after a couple of years. But sniff them, taste them, first – if they've lost their sparkle, ditch them.
- Go through your small appliances and get rid of any you no longer use.

CHAPTER THREE

Living

The heart of the matter

To be happy at home is the ultimate result
of all ambition, the end to which every
enterprise and labour tends.

SAMUEL JOHNSON

Living rooms can very easily become stuffed to the gills with unloved bits of inherited furniture, 'it'll-do-for-now' pieces, family memorabilia, half-done craft projects you're going to get to one day (Newsflash: you're not), photographs in search of albums, and children's drawings and toys. Papers and magazines sit fatly on tables; chairs play host to heaps of clothes that never quite made it into wardrobes; books spill off shelves; remote controls seem to have undertaken their own breeding programme somewhere over there in the corner. And this is the space where you're supposed to slough off the physical and emotional pummelling of the day and relax. Even worse, this is also the area of your home that your visitors see, bringing a whole new level of anxiety through the door, along with their not-quite-chilled-enough bottles of New Zealand sauv blanc.

I include hallways, staircases and landings in this chapter because these public arteries can also evolve into lively obstacle courses of casually discarded shoes, coats, bags, sports equipment and heaps of things which are on their way into the house, as well as heaps of things which are on the way out. They are also the first areas you see when you come home, so it's worth making an effort to keep them looking neat and welcoming to avoid that just-walked-in-the-door heart sink of doom.

A whole lot of livin' going on

One thing I have learned in the process of creating order and calm in my own house is that you can't go against the grain. The method I devised works for me because I shrugged off any sense of boring guilt at not being perfect at it to start with; I just got on with the job, muddling along and creating my own way, my own aesthetic. I hope that's what you'll do too.

I really started to fly when I forgot about all those flawless images on Pinterest and Instagram of one perfect table with one perfect jam jar and one perfect rose at

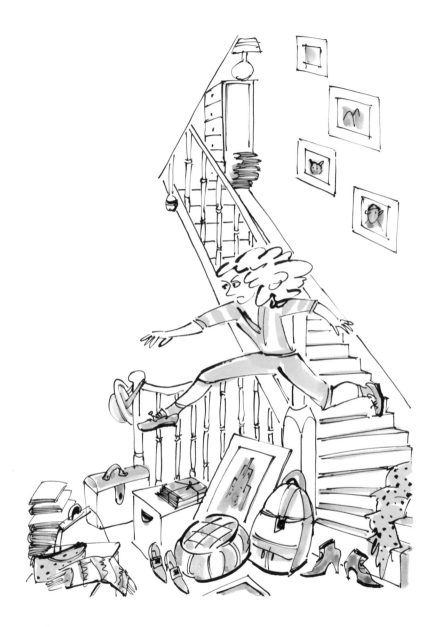

Hallways, staircases and landings can evolve into lively obstacle courses of casually discarded shoes, coats, bags, sports equipment.

the very second of peak blowsiness. I laughed in the face of those magazine features which, on the cover, promised to reveal the secrets of decluttering and then, when you turned to page 83, near-breathless with excitement that you may finally find the secret, the One Method to Rule Them All, only to discover, what? An exquisitely art-directed shot of a wardrobe which once contained 20 white linen shirts now pared back to ten. That's no good to me, pal, I thought, as I surveyed my own wardrobe, bursting with old sweaters I was keeping for gardening, dresses I would definitely wear just as soon as I found the right jacket, and shirts that had a good bit of wear in them yet once I got round to sewing on a few buttons.

I am going to share with you something really important now, something that is key to long-term success in Operation Declutter: don't attempt to circumvent your own personality type and expect to sustain your progress. Consider carefully exactly how you want to live, what will make you happy and what that will look like. Work slowly, persistently towards that, recalibrating and resetting your goals as you go. Keep it really personal.

This is where decluttering becomes a bit like dieting. Pretty much anyone can lose a chunk of weight quickly if we set our minds to it (drop a dress size by summer! and other madness). The challenge is keeping it off and creating the good habits that allow us to sustain the weight loss in the long term. On the declutter diet, find out what works for you and stick to it: nurture it, develop it and pat yourself on the back for every new success. That way, if you fall back at any point, it is much easier to forgive yourself (there's really nothing to forgive – you've just been busy being an actual real live human), throw that failure over your shoulder like so much spilled salt and begin again. That's it.

Here's what I know about living rooms

Start by thinking about how you use your living room. In your decluttering journal (see page 17), write down the various activities you use it for. Here is a typical activity list.

- Entertaining friends
- Watching television
- Reading
- Listening to or playing music
- Making things, crafts
- Household admin
- Exercise
- Family time
- Children playing or doing homework

In your journal, roughly sketch out the zones for each activity. I realize this may seem ridiculous if your sitting room is very small and you do a thousand different things in it, but this whole process is about seeing your space and your possessions in a new light and the act of sketching it out helps with that. Creating designated spaces to store things where you use them makes it so much more likely that you, and everyone else in your household, will put them away.

The first priority is to get stuff off the floor. Use baskets, shelves, trays and boxes to help you with this, but don't let them stagnate and just become more dumping grounds (see Coffee-cup zones, page 27). Cast your eyes over them each day during your Evening 15 (see page 134) and do a quick pick-up of anything that shouldn't be there. In addition, go through them properly each week to get rid of stuff that should go in the bin or in a different part of the house.

Storage by stealth is a great weapon in your decluttering armoury. Whenever you can, choose furniture that has some kind of storage built into it, particularly if your room is small. In our living room, we have a large trunk instead of a coffee table and we use it to store bedding for the sofa bed that sits next to it. Create window seats with cupboards beneath them and choose console tables that have shelves underneath, too. Cube-shaped seating and occasional tables with lift-off tops are good for toy storage (Ikea is usually pretty good for these). If your living space doubles as an office space, check out The Dormy House (thedormyhouse. com), particularly if you favour quite a trad English country-house style. They sell rather cunning ottomans which conceal hanging files for paperwork, and generous footstools with hinged lids – perfect for concealing things such as extra throws and board games. They will customize them to your own finish as well.

Small touches count, too. Make a designated place for remote controls which isn't behind the sofa cushions. Keep them in a bowl, basket or small tray so they're easy to find when you want them and easy to put back when you're finished.

TIP

Have wastepaper bins and recycling baskets in all your main rooms to make it as easy as possible to ditch the junk. If you have enough room, place more baskets on landings for objects that need to go out or go elsewhere.

When you can't look another bin bag in the eye...

Inevitably in this process – because for many of us it is a lengthy one – you will at some point fall into a massive sulk at the mere sight of another heap of stuff you need to sort through. So what do you do when you hit a slump but know you need to keep going? When I began working on this book, I asked my friend, food writer Julia Platt Leonard, how she keeps her house looking so calm and inviting, even though she, like me, has a ton of work-related stuff coming through the door each day. She said:

I declutter when it gets all too much – too many things on too many surfaces. It also creates pleasant spaces that are a pleasure to look at, and it makes me look at things afresh. Things I've had for years look better, brighter, more special because they're not competing for space and my attention with lots of other stuff.

I like Julia's eyes-on-the-prize attitude. Keep going so that you can really enjoy what remains after your purge, knowing it reflects your true tastes and makes you feel happy and uplifted to be home.

But what else can you do to keep you going?

○ Take a break. Do something you love for an hour or so. I'm a big fan of getting some fresh air as a way of refocusing my intentions, but you know best what works for you. Do that. For an hour. Then crack on.

o Stay in the moment. Break tasks down into doable components. For example, it may feel just too overwhelming to tackle all your books right now. Just tell yourself that today, right now, you are going to sort through your gardening books, or comic books, or whatever it is you have a decent heap of, and then you never need do that again.

o Your kitchen timer is your best friend (see page 34). Remember, the cumulative power of completing small tasks is mighty. Set your timer for 30 minutes. Tell yourself you will just do what you can until the buzzer goes off and then pat yourself on the back for getting going, even when you don't fancy it. If you've inspired yourself and you have the energy and time, have a break for ten minutes (five minutes is too short, 15 minutes potentially too long as you might end up getting distracted by pictures of toddlers falling in puddles on Twitter) and then do another 30-minute sort out. Repeat as necessary, but don't burn yourself out. It's really important not to put yourself off ever feeling able to tackle your clutter again and just resigning yourself to sleeping on a pillow of unmatched socks and that is fine thank you very much this is just how I live now what of it?

o Remind yourself an ordered home is easier to clean and tidy than a cluttered one. With every step, you are freeing yourself from ever needing to declutter on this scale again.

Hallways and stairways to heaven

Hallways are the first spaces visitors see but, more importantly, they're the first thing you see as you walk in the door. You want the entrance to your home to make you feel glad to be there, but keeping it clear and ordered is often a struggle. They have a lot of work to do in a limited space.

- Ideally, you need to create storage for coats, scarves, hats, gloves, umbrellas and sunglasses. Try to limit what you keep in the hall to stuff you'll be using this season to give yourself a fighting chance at order. Wellingtons, winter boots and heavy coats take up a lot of space, so if you're not wearing them daily try to find another spot for them until the weather turns.

- Some sort of bench seat with shelves underneath is a good idea if you have the room, as you can use it to store boots and shoes neatly. Cultivate the habit of extreme vigilance to prevent this important space becoming a dumping ground. A friend once asked me to admire a beautiful church pew she'd bought in an auction. It ran virtually the full length of her hallway, but I couldn't see it for bags, sports stuff and coats. I don't think anyone had sat on it since Wesley's first sermon.

I don't believe in failure. It's not failure if you enjoyed the process.
OPRAH WINFREY

- Try to make room for a mini recycling spot in the hall, so you can open the post and immediately dump anything you don't want into a basket or bin, ready to go out with the main recycling on your pick-up day.

- A row of pegs with shelves above give you somewhere to store hats and gloves as well as coats.

- If you have room in the hallway and/or landings for a large basket or two, this is a great place to keep the things you're decluttering until you can get them out of the house for good (make a note in your decluttering journal of exactly when you will do this).

- If you have dogs, put up a hook where you can hang leads and a bag with essential dog-walking supplies: poo bags; balls and other toys; treats; a whistle if you're that kind of person.

- Keep staircases clear. It's just flat out dangerous not to. If your Clutter Mountain has crept up the stairs, with every step becoming a shelf, begin your whole decluttering project here. It will make removing anything else later easier, less stressful and – most importantly – infinitely safer.

Kids' stuff

Modern children have 8 million toys each and that's just a fact. Wherever they play most – in living areas, their bedrooms, the kitchen – it will to reduce the Toynado Warning to mild if you can allocate a distinct area for their stuff. Create a corner with baskets, bins and some shelves, and encourage them to get into the habit of regular pick-ups – before meals or going out to play, for example. Making sure they know where their toys are supposed to go and teaching them great habits – to tackle

It will reduce the Toynado Warning to mild if you can allocate a distinct area for their stuff.

things when it's quick and easy to straighten them up – is an enormous kindness, even if it feels like a pain at the time.

I don't have kids, but I asked my best friend who has two lively boys and a busy life and a house that doesn't look like an explosion in a plastics factory how she manages to keep everything looking pulled together. These are her top tips:

- Have a trunk for the front room (like an old blanket box) so everything can be swept up and dumped in there when you need a quick, relatively stress-free clear-up.
- Add shelves for board games and toys, to keep them off the floor.
- Beware silly storage solutions that are too small and just end up becoming clutter themselves.
- And if all else fails, you can resort to regular yard sales. They're fun, kids love doing them and they are a brilliant decluttering solution

Other great tips I magpied from friends with children:

- Keep toys current and encourage the kids to give away anything they no longer play with. Try putting away some toys for a while to see if they miss them or ask for them. If they don't, it might be time to move them on.
- Discard anything that is broken, tatty or missing parts.
- Encourage activities that don't necessarily revolve around toys and more stuff.
- Be specific about what you expect from your children. 'Let's sort out the Lego' is more likely to get a result than 'We need to tidy up this mess!'

- Use your kitchen timer to make tidying up and decluttering into a race or a game. Doing a little each day is a great habit to get into, for everyone's sake.
- Sort like things together and create zones to make it as easy as possible for even quite small children to put their things away.
- Involve your children in the process of decluttering as much as you can. It will take longer but will benefit everyone in the long term. Younger children should still, wherever possible, help you to choose what to discard.
- Emphasize how you're freeing up more space to play and making it easier for them to be able to find the things they really like.
- Limit your own 'toys'. If they see you cluttering up the house with all the latest fads, indulging every whim and using it as excuse to load up with more stuff, they'll learn from what they see, not from what you say. Similarly, if they see you putting your possessions away – if it's the family norm – they're more likely to follow your lead.

Helping teenagers to declutter obviously presents a different set of requirements and expectations (see page 123).

It's raining cats' and dogs' toys

These days, even our pets come with a plethora of things: beds, toys, blankets, bowls, travel crates, collars and leads, second-best collars and leads, raincoats, even bootees.

- Get rid of pet toys that are past their best. They don't just look awful dotted about the house, but they can be dangerous, too, if bits break off that are large enough for your dog or cat to choke on.

Over the years I have bought quite a few luxurious dog and cat beds in which the animals themselves showed precisely zero interest.

- Collars become grubby quite quickly and many of them are impossible to clean. Replace them once they no longer look good.
- If you've crate-trained your dog and have decided you no longer want him or her to sleep in a crate, pass it on to a local animal rescue. They'll be delighted to have it.
- Ditch anything your pets don't like or use. Over the years, I have bought quite a few luxurious dog and cat beds in which the animals themselves showed precisely zero interest, preferring to stretch out on a favourite cushion or person. In the end I had to admit our artistic differences and pass these pristine and beautiful beds on to the local animal rescue.

The power of plants

Plants make a room look more welcoming to my eyes, but they're also something else to take care of, another responsibility if you're already feeling overwhelmed. Certainly, ditch plants like azaleas and gardenias. They might as well be treated like cut flowers, unless you have endless time and patience to give these pot-bound prima donnas exactly the sort of care and conditions they require. Still, there is so much research now, carried out by NASA no less, into the enormous power of plants to cleanse the air of toxins, that it's a pity to deprive yourselves of a few. For ease, stick to English ivy, peace lilies, spider plants and aloe vera, all of which are proper workhorses in the air-cleaning department and require precious little effort from you, other than the odd splash of water now and again. In bedrooms, moth orchids – once so exotic, but now very widely available - not only absorb carbon dioxide, but also release oxygen at night, helping to ensure a refreshing night's sleep.

Quick living area fixes

● If you have five minutes

○ Keep flat surfaces clear – sort out a coffee-cup zone (see page 27).

○ Take a quick spin around the living room and dispose of anything that is obviously rubbish; empty any wastepaper baskets.

○ Ditch any dead plants.

● If you have ten minutes

○ Go through a storage basket or tray and edit out anything that you don't need any more.

○ Sort through some books, newspapers and magazines. Put a few books in your donate pile by the door; put any newspaper more than a week old and any magazine more than a month old into the recycling.

○ Go through ornaments and photographs on surfaces and mantelpieces. Do you still love them? If not, move them on.

○ Consider how many of those throws and cushions you really need. If any of them are past their best or you just don't love them any more, give yourself the gift of never having to fold them or plump them up ever again. Either throw them out if they are too far gone, or donate them if they're just no longer to your taste.

○ Get the children to sort through some of their toys, books and games with you.

◑ If you have thirty minutes

○ You haven't looked at all those CDs and videos for years. Toss them or sell them; companies such as musicmagpie.co.uk (UK) or decluttr.com (US) are worth considering as you can get cash for old CDs, DVDs and games.

○ Go through any cupboards, large trunks or baskets and make sure you still want or need what's in them.

○ Sort through any piles of old photographs. Start creating albums for the ones you really like or put them in frames. It's fine to throw out photographs of: people you don't recognize; people you don't like; people you love who don't look great in that picture. Nothing bad will happen.

Calendar

Once a week

○ Ideally, do this once a day, but you know, sometimes life gets in the way. But once a week minimum go through all post, flyers and catalogues; file what you need to keep and recycle the rest.

Once a month

○ Get the children to go through their toys, games and books; throw out anything past its best and recycle anything they no longer use.

Every three to six months

○ Move outdoor wear that isn't in season out of the hallway.

○ Check any runners or rugs you have in hallways and sitting rooms or on landings to see if they need washing or specialist cleaning. Get rid of anything that's past its best.

Once a year

○ If you think you might enjoy it, plan a car-boot sale or yard sale. Include the children in this – there's something very motivating about discovering your old toys can make you money. It's fun sometimes to get together with neighbours or friends to do this too.

CHAPTER FOUR

Working and feeling

Less flotsam, more jetsam

Everything we do is infused with the energy with
which we do it. If we're frantic, life will be frantic.
If we're peaceful, life will be peaceful.

MARIANNE WILLIAMSON

Many of us have a space – or several spaces – in our homes given over to the paperwork and sundry flotsam of household admin, whether it's a small table tucked into the corner of a bedroom or a whole room dedicated to the machinery of keeping our lives, our jobs and our families on track.

When I began writing this chapter, I finally looked up flotsam in the dictionary. I'd been using it so much in my research notes that at one point I almost considered it as a name for our new puppy. I knew it had a distinctly different meaning to jetsam, its frequent sentence buddy. And lo, sometimes when you need something it will find you. Flotsam, from the French *flotter*, to float, is debris in the water that hasn't been deliberately thrown overboard. Jetsam refers to things that have been deliberately jettisoned, often in moments of extreme peril to lighten the load if the ship is in danger of sinking. This made me think that what we all need in this decluttering process is less flotsam mindlessly bobbing about and getting in the way of our true course, and more jetsam, cast off so we can continue safely on our journey. You don't need all this stuff. Chuck it overboard and save yourself.

Do your home work

So many of us work from home at least some of the time now and that brings with it a complex set of decluttering challenges. Even if you don't work from home, you still need an efficient space to keep on top of the necessary administration involved in keeping your particular show on the road. In a perfect world, you'd have a separate home office which would make it simple to close the door on work when you needed to, physically and emotionally. This isn't possible for many of us, so we have to find ways of metaphorically putting up a closed sign at the end of business hours. Getting your place in order helps tremendously with this. It's not restful

– and probably not very good for your digestion – to eat your dinner at a table covered in work stuff. It's much harder to unwind if the ephemera of your work day – notebooks, files, mail, spreadsheets – is cluttering your eyeline while you try to flip through a magazine, watch television, practise your Mongolian throat singing or do whatever it is you do to relax.

The tidy-enough desk

Everything starts from the desk, or whatever piece of furniture you're using as a desk. If it's crammed with files, folders, books, pots of pens, photographs and tchotchkes, it's going to be more difficult for you to concentrate. I mean, I love Penelope Garcia from *Criminal Minds* as much as the next murder-based thriller fan, but I don't know how she ever solves a crime with all those fairy lights, gonks, plastic unicorns, feathery pens and soft toys on her desk. Don't be like Penelope.

I am going to share with you the greatest tip I was ever given about organizing my desk. Get yourself a large cardboard box or plastic crate and put everything, absolutely everything, from your desk in there. You want a completely blank surface (give it a quick wipe while you're at it – desks can become Petri dishes of filth). Immediately, there will be things you need to put back on there: your computer; a lamp; a notebook and a pen; your phone. See how long you can go without needing anything else. Enjoy the calm and space. If this is your main desk – where you work every day – after a couple of days, anything you haven't required from the box of stuff is not essential to your working life and should be stored elsewhere, in file boxes or on shelves. If your main office is away from your home and you only use this desk from time to time, you can extend that grace period for up to ten days.

Of course, the Desk Zero look may be perfect for you, or you may want a few embellishments if it feels too extreme – uncluttered shouldn't mean uninviting.

You don't need all this stuff. Chuck it overboard and save yourself.

I have a fern (particularly good for purifying the air around computers, also looks nice, see page 96), two small framed photographs and a jar of dog treats for the two canine office assistants who sleep under my desk.

If you have room, keep a small bookcase or crate next to your desk for files and books associated with current projects. Move them on when each project is done.

Once you've got your desk looking shipshape, get cracking on the rest of the space. At least now you have somewhere neat from which to survey your empire (spare bedroom) and plan further world domination.

Create a workspace that works

- Go through all your paperwork and recycle or shred everything you can before you even think about losing your head in Paperchase. Keep to a system: sort, then toss, then store.
- Scan anything you don't need a physical copy of and store it electronically (see page 112).
- Invest in a shredder for sensitive documents. If you have small children or pets, make sure you keep it on a high surface or unplugged when you're not using it. Most of them start working automatically when something's inserted in the slot, which can be catastrophic for tiny fingers or long, silky ears. A lot of councils won't accept shredded paper in their kerb-side recycling, so check with yours before putting it out.

- After you've properly purged your work area, decide how best you're going to store the things you absolutely have to keep there. Use vertical storage such as shelves, cabinets, bookcases, peg boards, cork boards and wall-mounted storage units as much as you can to maximize your space. If you're using a shared part of your home to work in, try to choose pieces that allow you to conceal the busy-ness of business, as this will create a calmer space after hours. This is particularly important if your work space is, unavoidably, in your bedroom.
- Ditch any outdated technology (hardware or software), and anything that doesn't work perfectly. There are many not-for-profit organizations that will collect and recycle some e-waste, though not many of them are nationwide and some just handle commercial stuff. Start with weeecharity.co.uk or Google for one that's near you. Make sure you've deleted all your personal data.
- Go through all your cables and electrical cords. Make sure you know what they're all for and get rid of any that you no longer use. If you're tempted to save any of them because they might come in useful one day, remind yourself of the space they're taking up and how cheaply you can probably replace them if you need to.
- Go through your office drawers. Only keep in them the things you need within arm's reach. Once you have sorted through them, use drawer dividers to keep everything neat.

Book boot camp

Even when many of us have cheerfully hopped on board the decluttering bus, we're pulling the emergency cord and begging to jump off at the first mention of casting out our books. Why is that? Why are they so much more emotionally loaded than our other possessions, and why are we so resistant to even considering them clutter?

A few years ago, our friends Denise and Vicky needed to make room in their flat for their new business, so they sold or donated thousands of their books, leaving only a dozen or so hefty art books on a sturdy shelf. I was surprised at how shocked I was at this revolutionary act against middle-class values, but then I *was* Camus-flage Girl (see page 30).

Vicky, who is one of the calmest people you'll ever meet – the sort of person you'd want next to you in the bunker – explained, 'We needed the space more than we needed the books. If I ever want to read any of them again, I can just buy them or download them.'

Most of us buy far more books than we will ever read, and often the ones we leave languishing on the shelf are those that, deep down, we bought to reflect the kind of person we think we ought to be. There's no 'ought'. Live your own life, not a pale imitation of someone else's (scoop: they're probably not living that life either).

- Books don't define you as a person. Love the ones you love and read them. The rest is just shopping.
- If you decide to sell your books rather than donate them, bear in mind that most paperbacks have very little resale value. Consider how much time and space you will have to dedicate to them for relatively small financial reward.
- Limber up by discarding the easy ones – out-of-date reference books, small travel dictionaries (use your phone, obviously), gifts

from people who don't know your taste, thrillers you have read so you know the ending, holiday books you're unlikely to read more than once (reader, after a few bumps in the road and poor wardrobe choices, she married him).

o Quickly scan your shelves and pick out ten books that people you love will enjoy. Give them to them. Do this as often as you can. Add books into your 30-day declutter challenge (see page 56) and, if you have loads of them, consider doing a 30-day challenge exclusively on your books.

o Of course, you can drop off your books at charity shops, or you could create a tiny free library in your neighbourhood – simply a small waterproof bookcase in a public place where people can take and leave books as they wish. Check out littlefreelibrary.org for how to join the 60,000 people worldwide who've done just that.

o When considering new books, think about downloading ones you're only likely to read once, rather than buying an actual copy you'll have to schedule for decluttering in 18 months' time.

o Like everything in this process, the more you do it the easier it gets, so keep going and don't be discouraged if you find it difficult at first.

Getting personal

Decluttering's high priestess, Marie Kondo, suggests people should declutter in this order: clothes first, then books, then papers, then *komono* (miscellany) and then sentimental things. This makes perfect sense. Only a fool would run a marathon without doing any training first. You need to build up to the really juicy stuff lurking in your bureau and desk drawers and long-forgotten boxes in attics and under beds.

- Remember, you aren't ditching the person, the memory, the experience, the feeling, you're just getting rid of their physical manifestation in the form of photographs, letters, pictures and other heart-tugging totems.
- Kondo recommends focusing on what you want to keep rather than what you need to throw away. This shift in perspective is particularly important when it comes to sentimental things. Keep the best, the pieces that really make your heart sing, and ditch the rest.
- Check out the principles of Swedish death cleaning (see page 22) and keep in your mind the question, 'Will anyone be happier if I save this?'
- Articles in vintage magazines and on websites and blogs will sometimes tell you that repurposing items to which you have a strong sentimental attachment is a good way of breathing new life into them. By all means, fashion your grandpa's old tweed jacket into a cushion, or transform your daughter's baby dresses into a patchwork quilt if you have the time and inclination, but be very honest with yourself about how likely you are to do this. Set a time limit and, if you haven't done it by then, move them on.
- Getting rid of children's paintings, drawings and other forms of artistic expression can be really tough, because it feels as if you're rejecting Essence of Child. Of course, you're not. This is one of the occasions when it's a great idea to get the children to help you sort through their stuff. It's almost guaranteed they're not nearly as attached to their pictures as you are. Have them help you

choose their favourite two, or three, or five, or whatever feels like a comfortable number to you, and frame them or display them in some way that honours them. Take photographs of any of the others you're particularly fond of and then dispatch the originals to art heaven.

Don't opt in for overload

Embrace your inner no, cherish it, nurture it and bring it out to play. You know that feeling when someone asks you to go somewhere, do something, help with an event and – just as you feel your heart sinking – out of your mouth trip the words, 'Of course! Happy to.' Stop doing that.

I get it. It's really hard sometimes, particularly if you're an inveterate people pleaser. (I am. In recovery, but I definitely am, thank you for listening.) But practise paying attention to that heart sink. It will seldom steer you wrong. Physical clutter often hitches a ride on the back of mental clutter, the symptoms of which are over-committing yourself and tiring yourself out. Prioritise your own equilibrium. 'No' is a complete sentence, as they say, and there are plenty of things we all have to do without opting in for overload. Being a loyal friend, neighbour and colleague is good, but being loyal to your own dear and lovely self is better.

Creativity involves breaking out of established patterns in order to look at things in a different way.

EDWARD DE BONO

Declutter your brain

Get into the habit of jotting down your domestic thoughts as they pop into your head, along with an approximate time when you might complete any niggling tasks (see page 17). This puts the brakes on 'whirling dervish brain', which can be paralyzing. One of the things I love most about a list is the satisfaction of crossing things off as I go along. It's so supremely motivating. In fact, I sometimes write things on my list that I've already completed for the pure pleasure of crossing them off. And I suggest you do the same – anything to help you realize how far you have come is absolutely A Good Thing. Remember never to let planning get in the way of action, though. There's nothing more dynamic than doing. Lists are fine, but activity brings with it its own energy. It's better to clear a few folders in your filing cabinet than to spend an hour on the perfect list.

Virtual clutter

As online email services offer more and more free digital storage – well, in exchange for a few adverts on your sidebar – the temptation to keep every single email is strong. Then you try to find a particular email and your search returns several hundred that match your search words. Or your mailbox regularly gets so full it starts to reject any new messages.

To tidy your inbox, sort your emails by sender and remove those that are no longer (or were never) relevant. Then sort by date and delete any ancient emails you really don't need to keep. Get into the habit of doing this regularly. Similarly, if your computer desktop is cluttered with files, delete those partial drafts long since completed, and file the rest in your computer storage. This will make opening your device a much calmer experience.

I sometimes write things on my list that I've already completed for the pure pleasure of crossing them off.

Digital storage

There are several ways to store documents electronically, either locally on your device or remotely online. The easiest to use is the range of note-taking applications, such as Microsoft OneNote, Evernote, Simplenote and Google Keep. Many of these are free, and work on desktops and mobiles. They let you store typed notes, web clippings, electronic documents and pictures in customizable filing systems. Some have an app for your mobile as well – ideal for information you might want at short notice or when you're away from home, such as driving licence details, copies of your MOT or car, travel or home insurance. With any of these systems, investigate comprehensive back-up – such as Cloud storage – in case of a digital disaster, but again, many of them have incorporated this function.

There are many commercial systems that allow the systematic scanning of all your documents so that you can throw the paper ones away (hurray!). You'll need a scanner with a document feeder, but doing this will certainly cut down on physical paperwork, and these systems help you sort and store the scanned files, too.

How to store physical documents

When you've been through all your paperwork, purged anything you don't need and digitized everything you can digitize, you need to create a system for physical paperwork that makes it easy to put things away and to retrieve them when you need them. Keep it simple – otherwise you'll be tempted to avoid your filing and admin until it's actually blocking out all natural light.

- The first rank of documents are those that are difficult to replace. Keep birth and marriage certificates, share certificates, wills, deeds and mortgage papers together in a safe place.
- If you work from home, you may need a filing cabinet with hanging files, but for most of us a few ring binders and/or box files will do.
- Add transparent plastic wallets and label them. You can colour-code them if you like, too, as this makes them even easier to retrieve: green for utility bills, blue for bank statements, red for phone bills and so on. Make a separate folder for things like appliance guarantees, car documents and insurance policies, and another one, or a file box, for appliance manuals.
- File your existing paperwork in the wallets, in reverse chronological order so that the most recent documents are on top.
- When new bills come in, if you don't have time to file them straight away, place them in another pending wallet or filing tray, but do go through them at least once a week and put them in their appropriate wallets. Scribble 'paid' or 'dealt with' on the top of anything that you've paid or dealt with.

Divide each difficulty into as many parts
as necessary to resolve it.
RENÉ DESCARTES

When can you ditch stuff?

○ You should hold onto bank statements and bills for at least two years and insurance documents and guarantees for as long as they are valid.

○ Currently, HMRC (gov.uk) advises holding onto tax paperwork such as pay slips, P45s and so on for at least 22 months from the end of the tax year they relate to. In the US, the IRS recommends keeping records relating to your taxes for three years.

○ If you run your own business, keep all your bills, receipts and other financial documentation for five years after you've filed your taxes in case you're audited. That means that paperwork you've filed to meet the 31 January 2019 submission date for the tax year 2017–18, you'll need to hold onto until at least 31 January 2024.

TIPS

● Take some distraction action if you find being constantly plugged into social media is draining you of energy or fuelling your procrastination. Delete the apps from your phone, or hide them so they're not the first thing you see, or use an app blocker. Try giving yourself some unplugged time to recharge your own batteries.

● To cut down on financial paperwork, sign up for online bank statements and utility bills wherever you can. Stop all that paper from coming in the door in the first place.

Quick work area fixes

● If you have five minutes

○ Keep flat surfaces clear – sort out a coffee-cup zone (see page 27).

○ Sort through the post and put things you need to file in the relevant folder.

○ Remove anything on your noticeboard that is no longer important – don't let it stagnate.

◑ If you have ten minutes

○ Go through a storage basket or tray and edit out anything you don't need any more.

○ Sort through some books, newspapers and magazines. Put a few books in your donate pile by the door; put any newspaper more than a week old and any magazine more than a month old into the recycling.

○ Go through some of your kids' artwork with them and decide together what you want to keep.

◐ If you have thirty minutes

○ Clear off your desk completely. Only allow back on it things you use all the time. If you haven't time to create new homes for your desk orphans right away, scribble a time in your decluttering journal (see page 17) to get to that.

○ Clear your digital desktop. Delete drafts you're no longer working on, file completed documents and downloaded pictures and gifs you want to hang onto.

Calendar

Once a week

○ Sort all filing; discard anything you no longer need to keep.

○ Check your desk space for any extraneous items that have crept back onto it.

○ Sort and clear your email and digital desktop.

○ Check your coffee-cup zones (see page 27) for stray documents that need filing.

Once a month

○ Sort through any receipts or other materials you will need for your tax return so it's not a mad dash at deadline time.

Every three to six months

○ Ditch any manuals for appliances you no longer own.

Once a year

○ Go through bills, receipts, bank statements and other sensitive financial paperwork and shred it.

○ Clear out any expired insurance documents and warranties.

○ Throw out, sell or recycle any small electrical kit that you haven't used for a year.

CHAPTER FIVE

Sleeping, dressing and relaxing

The great unwind

You don't always have to be doing something.
You can just be, and that's plenty.

ALICE WALKER

Often the room in your home that should be the most nurturing and restful is the source of most anxiety. Clothes burst out of wardrobes, second-best bathrobes slump gloomily on hooks, unread magazines and paperbacks clutter nightstands, nests of odd socks colonize valuable drawer space, and chairs groan under the weight of yesterday's (or last week's) clothes.

Sometimes the fact that it is only us, and those we are most intimate with, who ever see our bedrooms means these spaces are unshackled from the sense of gnawing obligation that drives us to keep the rest of the house in reasonable order (see Is your home skinny fat?, page 46), so they can be a particular challenge. This also means they can be a particular source of shame, too. But shame is something that always stands in the way of progress, so you can shrug that off right now. Not needed on voyage.

What's your intention, as Oprah would say? I think what most of us require from our bedrooms is that they are somewhere we can be our most unguarded and vulnerable selves, where we can relax completely, sleep deeply and, in the morning, prepare ourselves calmly for the day ahead. This is why good hotel bedrooms are so calming (see page 15): they contain the minimum required for civilised existence. Grab your decluttering journal (see page 17) and write down what your intention is for your bedroom. For once, I think this should be a very short list: sleeping, recharging (however that manifests itself for you) and dressing. The end.

You're not going to have the sort of sleep that really 'knits up the ravell'd sleeve of care' in a muddle. Your room doesn't have to look like something from Pinterest – in fact, I think the very idea of aiming for someone else's highly stylised aesthetic puts undue pressure on you and is a waste of time. Order has its own beauty. A clean, aired, well-organized bedroom with clear surfaces and a freshly made bed is one of the most soul-pleasing and nurturing places on the planet. You can create that for yourself, right now.

Remember when we talked about how, in your home office, everything starts with the desk (see page 102)? In the bedroom, everything begins with the bed. Making your bed every day is the kindest thing that Morning You can do for Evening You. However rushed you are (my husband and I have an agreement that the person who gets up last has to make the bed, so there's an incentive to be an early riser, right there), the couple of minutes it takes is worth it when in the evening you come home to a comfortable bed, not a tangle of sheets. So start with that and build out from there.

And so to bed

A few years ago, I saw a piece in *Martha Stewart Living* magazine on organizing your bedlinen with each set – fitted sheet, top sheet if you use one, duvet cover, pillowcases – folded inside a pillowcase from the same set, so that they could be stored in a simple parcel of time-saving beauty. My friend, gardening writer Laetitia Maklouf, tweeted a picture of her own linens arranged this way and it was an image of such pleasing tranquillity, I actually invited myself over to take a look. I can highly recommend this method, particularly if you are short on storage space. With my own linens, I store them in a cupboard and label the edges of the shelves: king-size fitted sheets, king-size duvet, double top sheets, rectangular pillowcases, square pillowcases and so on. It's all white, so everything goes with everything else – all I have to do is a quick pick-and-mix every week when I change the bed.

- You only need two, possibly three, sets of bedlinen per bed. You only really need three sets for children's beds if they're still of the age where they might have accidents or get sick in the night.

- If you have bedlinen that is all the same colour, everything goes with everything else. White is fresh and restful, but of course you can use other colours, too, or families of coordinated colours if you like a more eclectic look.

- Take a look at your bed. Have you Pinterested the hell out of it, with lots of extra cushions and pillows and throws? That's lovely, of course – if it makes you feel happy every day – but do bear in mind that it adds a few extra minutes' work each morning when you're making your bed and creates extra laundry. Consider paring it back to a simpler look that's still comfortable and attractive but less of a time suck.

- Cut old, unused sheets into rags for cleaning and shoe polishing, but be realistic about how many you need. No one needs a cupboard full of dusters. Homelessness charities and cold-weather projects are often grateful for used bedding in good condition (only give them things that you would be happy to sleep on and under yourself).

Children's bedrooms

I've written elsewhere about banishing the tyranny of too many toys (See Kids' stuff, page 89) and the challenge of decluttering with teenagers (See Sharing isn't always caring, page 53) but some of these points bear reiterating here. There are some particular difficulties when it comes to helping them with their own spaces, but the key point, and the one that if you follow it will get you further than anything else, is the example you set by your own behaviour. Sometimes it seems as if we expect more from children than we do of ourselves, perhaps because it's easier to badger them than to address our own shabby habits (welcome to an Introduction to Psychology everyone, today's subject is transference). This comes into particularly sharp focus with teenagers, who not only see all but certainly know all. Shore up your defences by at least beginning to tackle your own disordered spaces before you expect them to do the same.

- However small the space, even if it's shared with a sibling – in fact, probably especially if it is shared with a sibling – it's a good idea to get them to sketch out the space (or do it for them if they are very small) and work out where the various activities we expect from children's bedrooms to take place: sleeping, playing, studying, relaxing. Try to group together the objects required for these things in the area where they are used to make it as easy as possible to put them away.

- Most children thrive in ordered spaces. Wherever you can, have crates, shelves and drawers to help them keep their rooms neat. Don't get too hung up on a picture-perfect scheme, just something that's practical and easy to use. You might want to colour code crates to help smaller children to help themselves – blue for soft toys, green for arts-and-crafts materials and so on.

- Involve them in Operation Tidy Up from the beginning, in a way that's appropriate for their age. If they have a sense of ownership, they're more likely to pick up the good habits you'd like them to acquire, along with their toys.

- Even quite small children can help keep their rooms looking pulled together and neat if you make it as easy as possible for them to do it successfully. Encourage them to make their beds each day – it's easy to shake a duvet and plump up a pillow, and it doesn't matter if they don't do it perfectly. Try to get them to put dirty clothes in the laundry basket and keep the floor reasonably clear.

- With children, Marie Kondo's approach of asking them what they would like to keep rather than what they would like to throw away seems to work particularly well. Stay focused on what you are creating (more room to play with their friends, to do their homework peacefully and so on) rather than what you are getting rid of.

- A dynamic approach of asking them, 'Where does this live?' sometimes works better than 'Clear this up!'

- Do the easy stuff first to help build up a sense of achievement – empty wastepaper bins, dump dirty clothes in laundry baskets, pick up things that are scattered on the floor, recycle clothes that are obviously far too small, throw out anything that is broken.

- Break things down into small tasks. Encourage children to tackle a shelf, a drawer or a box at a time. Set the timer to make it into a game if you think that would help. Consider a sticker chart for very small children so they can appreciate how far they have come. (In fact, I wouldn't mind a sticker chart for myself if I'm honest.)

- If a 15 Fling (see page 66) is too much of a challenge, encourage small children to get into the habit of doing a 5 Fling on a fairly frequent basis. Creating good habits is far more important and

and successful in the long run than one-off blitzes which are exhausting and fray everyone's nerves.

o With teenagers, try and get them to do a 30-day declutter challenge (see page 56), either independently or alongside one you're doing. They often enjoy this, particularly if they're the types who like to share things on social media.

o Obviously, teenage bedrooms can be disaster zones, but it's never more important to tread carefully than it is in these areas. A growing sense of independence, privacy and boundaries makes any intervention from you particularly tricky. Do everything you can to help them make their spaces clean and ordered, but know when to pick your battles (see Sharing isn't always caring page 53). It may be that you need to agree that they do their bit in the shared parts of the home, loading the dishwasher, hanging up their coats and so on, but their rooms are their own domain so long as they aren't completely rancid.

Out with hatred, in with love

I've mentioned before that I'm not one of life's meditators. I'm not good at sitting still, I always have my eye on the next thing and I'm usually last to leave the party because I can't bear the thought of missing anything.

I am sure this is why I ended up with too much stuff. I didn't let myself slow down long enough to separate what I wanted rightnowthisminute from what I truly needed. I really hesitate to bring mindfulness into this, as the whole concept has been tarnished by those chia-seeding-flax-grinding-charcoal-activating mega bores too busy hand-looming their own sense of moral superiority to remember to smile.

'...those chia-seeding-flax-grinding-charcoal-activating mega bores too busy hand-looming their own sense of moral superiority to remember to smile.'

But. But. I started going to my meditation classes and I learned to stay with my breath, still my thoughts, focus on the moment and give my brain a rest. It really helped with my decluttering because it stopped the exhausting internal monologue that went something like this:

Today's the day! I'm going to fling open the windows and finally sort out the sitting room. Shouldn't take too long. But what am I going to do with all those books? And that little table I bought in the junk shop with the wobbly leg? I suppose I can fix that. But no, I can't get the tool box out of the cellar without scaling Mount Laundry and attempting to traverse tricky What's The Point? I'm hopeless at this. Oh well, the sun is out, seems a shame to miss it. Perhaps I'll take the dogs to the park and get to this tomorrow. First thing. Definitely. I bet I'd have time to do the dining room, too, if I really put my mind to it.

Sound familiar? My teacher Linda holds classes in London, but you can find them online on her own site (audiomeditation.co.uk) and on YouTube, too. Other sources of inner peace you might like to try are Buddhify (buddhify.com), Headspace (headspace.com) and Calm (calm.com).

By having less and doing more, we will be happier, healthier, richer, in every sense: less clutter, less regret, less anxiety, more meaning, more flow, more intrinsic enjoyment, better conversations, more connections, a healthier take on status, and a stronger sense of belonging.

JAMES WALLMAN

And not a thing to wear ...

In this country we throw out a staggering 300,000 tonnes of used clothes every year – it's hardly surprising, when fashions change so quickly and often clothes are so cheap they might as well be disposable.

It's all very well preaching quality over quantity, but that tends to fall on deaf ears when the exact perfect top for that party tonight is a tenner in the supermarket or charity shop. And, of course, being British, I can't just take a compliment. If anyone says they like my top, I practically do a lap of honour around the kitchen screaming, 'Only a tenner at Asda! I win! I win!' Which of course, I do, in a way. But whatever the bargain, that feeling of victory fades for all of us when we are once again standing in front of our over-stuffed wardrobes contemplating why we have so many clothes and nothing at all we want to wear. It's time to get rid of the ballast and pare back to the things we really love.

This is what I've gleaned from sorting the wheat from the chaff in my own wardrobe:

- Do not, whatever you do, dump everything on the bed all at once. You may never dig yourself out. Define what you will be able to do today, in this session, so you know what success looks like.

- Go through your underwear drawer and throw out anything old, grubby, worn out, holey or ill-fitting. This may leave you with three pairs of pants and a bra, but at least you know where you stand (in clean socks).

- I like this tip from Peter Walsh, Oprah's home-organization guru, though it works best if you've already done a fairly rigorous sort through of your wardrobe and are at the stage of refining and editing what you've got. He suggests taking all the hangers in your wardrobe and turning the clothes around so the hook part faces outwards. During the next six months, every time you return something to your wardrobe, put the hanger back the other way, so at a glance you have a strong idea which clothes you really wear and which ones you just think you wear.

- Do a quick appraisal of anything you think you like, but for some reason never seem to wear. Is it itchy? Does the label scratch your neck? Does it sit oddly across your shoulders or crease into a rag after ten minutes' wearing? If the things that make you avoid wearing a piece can be fixed, fix them. If not, get rid of any item that doesn't make you feel really good when you put it on.

- We all need a few things to wear when doing particularly mucky tasks around the house or garden, such as painting the ceiling or turning over the compost heap. A few. Not 20 T-shirts and ten stretched-out pairs of sweat pants. The majority of household jobs are perfectly do-able in your ordinary clothes. Allow yourself one, maximum two, sets of clothes for grubby work.

- You are never going to love any piece of clothing more than you love it right this minute. Think about whether or not you would buy it if you saw it hanging in a shop right now, in exactly the same condition. If the answer is no, get rid of it.

- Cut down on multiples. No one needs 20 white shirts. Get rid of any that are past their best.

- Take a look at your shoes and boots. Immediately discard anything that pinches, is uncomfortable or makes you walk like a drunken goat. Life really is too short to have painful feet.

- Sort, toss, recycle, donate. Make sure clothes that you're taking to the charity shop are clean and in good nick (see page 40). Don't pass on your own chaos by giving them your junk; it's just another form of procrastination.
- Check out loveyourclothes.org.uk for advice on mending, revamping and recycling your clothes.
- When you've been through your wardrobe and really pared it down, make a note in your decluttering journal (see page 17) of anything that would genuinely fill a gap and give the clothes you already have in your wardrobe a new lease of life – a certain jacket that would be great with a whole load of skirts and trousers, for example. This helps curb impulse buying and makes sure that the purchases you do make are carefully considered and will actually be useful to you.

Bags, wallets and purses

Think of them as the filing cabinets you carry around with you every day. Keep them in good order and, in the course of a year, it'll save you masses of time and stress. I read a report once that said women spend approximately ten minutes a day riffling through their handbags. That's more than an hour a week, 52 hours a year, when you could be doing something you enjoy. You will also reduce all manner of shoulder, back and neck pain which results from lugging half your life about with you on a daily basis.

- As you did with your desk (see page 100), start by taking everything out of your bag and working out exactly what needs to be there. For most of us, the basics will include keys, phone, wallet,

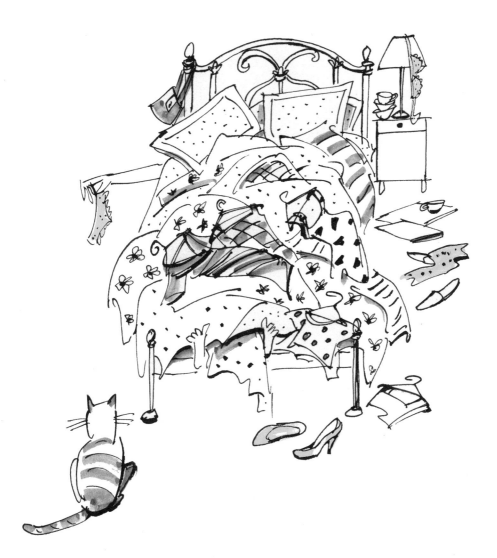

Do not, whatever you do, dump everything on the bed all at once.

any security passes we need to go about our daily business and a brush or comb. Extras might include a small make-up bag pared back to its essentials. For some of us (me), that might only be a lipstick or a lip balm. You may also need glasses and/or sunglasses, hand cream, tissues, headphones, a notebook and pen, a bottle of water and your laptop.

- You can buy bag organizers which mean you can transfer the essentials from one bag to another without tipping everything out and starting again. I don't care for these mainly because I think it's a really good thing to tip everything out and start again (editing, always editing), but also because most of my bags are such different shapes and sizes, it seems like a tremendous faff for precious little benefit.

- Get into the habit of going through your bag at the end of each day and getting rid of anything that's obviously rubbish (old ticket stubs, grubby tissues, gummy pens, crumpled-up Post-it notes, sweetie papers). Creating a clear canvas for tomorrow is an enormous kindness to yourself.

- Do the same with your wallet or purse, discarding loyalty cards, store cards and credit or debit cards you don't use (I feel I have to tell you to do this with an eye to security, but I know you already know that), any business cards once you've recorded the useful details on your phone, any old receipts (or file them away if you need them for expenses). Get into the habit of declining receipts for small things such as cups of coffee and newspapers. They just gum up your wallet.

What to do with glasses?

Glasses you no longer wear or with a prescription that no longer matches your requirements can be recycled. In the UK Vision Aid Overseas uses the money they make from recycling the glasses' components to support eye-care programmes in developing countries. Check their website (visionaidoverseas.org) for opticians all over the country where you can donate. (Try saving-sight.org in the US).

The life-changing power of passing it on

I am sure you are a good and loyal friend and that is a highly admirable quality in a human being. It's not so great when it extends to your wardrobe, though. Sometimes we hang onto clothes because of their associations – you wore an expensive outfit to a wedding or special party, and though you might never wear it again, you feel reluctant to let it go. We've spoken a lot about being able to give away possessions and still hold onto the special memories associated with them, so you know all of that by now. If you need an extra push to pass along your good things, consider smartworks. org.uk. This UK organization helps women in need with clothes, training and advice to prepare them for job interviews. Suitedbootedcentre.org.uk provides the same help for men. In the US, similar services are provided by dressforsuccess.org and careergear.org. That suit you never wear sitting in your wardrobe right now might genuinely help change someone's life.

If you needed this right now, where would you look for it?

Don't ask yourself where you should look for it – whatever *it* is – but where, out of habit, you do look for it. We all organize slightly differently. This is a bespoke system, built around you, and only you know your own logical processes. For example, I keep my tweezers and a rather terrifying, tiny magnifying mirror in my desk drawer, as I quite enjoy ramping up the tension while I'm waiting for a stressy email or phone call by plucking my eyebrows. I keep my dog-grooming kit in a little bag in the sitting room, as the only time I can get our puppy Gracie to sit still long enough to be brushed is when we're cosied up together watching television in the evening. If you can never put your hand on something when you need it, consider storing it in the place where you use it rather than where you think it 'ought' to go.

Finding a declutter companion

Our homes are three-dimensional representations of our inner lives. Those who practise feng shui (see page 20) believe we're connected to every single thing we own by tiny, invisible, emotional threads. So far, so exhausting.

Why not just free ourselves? There are many reasons why we are loath to let go, not least the Endowment Effect, a phrase coined by economist Richard Thaler to describe how we irrationally ascribe a greater value to objects simply because we own them. They might be worthless to anyone else, but to us they are treasures (almost) beyond price.

This emotional attachment we have to our own stuff is the reason it's so much easier to help someone else discard their possessions than it is to do it for ourselves. It can be really effective to get someone else along to help you out. Perhaps you could offer to return the favour, too?

- Be careful who you choose. Asking that stylish friend who is hilarious at dinner but then goes all Mean Girls when presented with your wardrobe is certainly one of the most effective ways to declutter Ms Fashionable Funny from your life forever.
- Try to find someone who is kind but who has a determined edge to them, too. You need someone with whom you feel comfortable

discussing any feelings that bubble to the surface, but who will chivvy you on through the tears. For perfection, some sort of latter-day Mary Poppins. Spit spot!

○ Ask for what you want. Be specific. Do you want someone who will be quite strict with you? Someone who will just hold your hand and keep you going while you make most of the decisions yourself? How do you want them to handle it if you really disagree about something?

○ Set a time limit and set your expectations: this way you know when you have succeeded. For example, suggest you give yourselves two hours, plus tea, to declutter your winter clothes, or go through shoes, scarves, accessories and make-up.

○ Get your friend to divide your things up between donate and ditch. If they bag them up as you go along, you're less likely to have second thoughts.

○ Having a friend along can help with that fear that you'll regret giving something up. They can help you focus on clearing the way for better things.

Above all, be the heroine of your own life, not the victim.

NORA EPHRON

Curb your enthusiasm

I see you, with your posh storage catalogue. I see you because I have been you, sitting there with my cup of coffee, Lakeland catalogue and block of Post-it notes, trying to convince myself that if I buy that crate, that magazine box or those drawer dividers, the job's as good as done.

It really isn't. If sorting out your home were a cake, sourcing the sundry smart storage gubbins would be the equivalent of sprinkles on the top. Before you get to that bit, you need to sort and toss. Sort and toss. I can't say this forcefully enough. I'll say it again: sort and toss. It's only when you've pared down your belongings to your own comfort level that there's any point in rewarding yourself with more stuff, however decorative and supposedly 'useful' it might be. Don't buy a shoe rack for 30 pairs of shoes before you realize you only own ten pairs that you actually wear and like.

The Evening 15

Struggling by on too little sleep is a modern epidemic and it makes tackling Clutter Mountain so much more daunting. In fact, studies indicate that those with a high risk of hoarding show evidence of poor sleep. Don't sabotage yourself by staying up until the small hours sorting out heaps of junk. It may, fleetingly, make you feel triumphant, but the next day will be a struggle and you're less likely to keep going. Late in the evening is not the time to embark on big decluttering tasks, but there are some things you can do to make the morning easier.

Personally, I hate that feeling of staying up too late to go to bed 'properly', waiting until I'm so tired I end up puttering about longer than I should because I just can't bear the thought of all the admin – brushing teeth, cleansing and moisturising my weary face, putting the dogs outside for wees, locking the doors, setting the alarm. I'm not exaggerating when I say that one of the most transformative things I've done for my adult self is to start the process of going to bed earlier, rather than waiting until I'm already exhausted. And one of the reasons I now give myself more time is so that I can squeeze in my Evening 15, as a gift to my morning self. Completing just a few fairly straightforward tasks each evening gets the following day off to a much less stressful start. I do as much of the following as I can face in 15 minutes:

- Fold some laundry
- Load the dishwasher and clear the draining board of stuff
- Wipe down the kitchen surfaces and sink
- Empty a wastepaper basket and/or chuck something into the recycling bin
- Fix any packed lunches
- Straighten up the sofa and plump up the cushions
- Pack keys, books, passes – anything I might need in the morning
- Charge my phone and laptop
- Put out my clothes for the next day. This might be my favourite, most life-enhancing one. Who wants to make aesthetic decisions at 7am?

Quick sleeping and dressing area fixes

If you have five minutes

○ Go through your bag and get rid of anything you don't need. If you do this in the evening, once you've finished decluttering it, add anything you need for the next day.

○ Do the same with your purse or wallet.

○ Sort through your jewellery and return anything on your dressing table to the place where you store it. Take a moment to consider whether or not you still want to hang onto it.

○ Check that any moth treatments you're using are up to date.

If you have ten minutes

○ Do a speedy wardrobe sweep. Either donate, give away or throw out anything you no longer love or that is past its best.

○ Tidy up your dressing table and nightstand. Get rid of anything past its best, remove books, magazines and papers you've read to their permanent homes, or recycle them.

If you have thirty minutes

○ Look through your shoes and boots. Think about the ones you still enjoy wearing. Pass on anything you no longer love. Give the ones that remain a good polish, and take anything that needs repairing to the cobbler's.

Calendar

Once a week

o Put aside anything that needs mending, new buttons, a hem taking up and so on. Try to do it right away. If you haven't done it within a month, consider how much you really need to keep that piece if you can do without it for so long.

o When you're putting away your laundry, make sure each sock has found its mate. Don't just stuff odd socks in the drawer and hope they will sort it out among themselves.

Once a month

o Turn your mattress. Sort through your bedlinen and move on anything stained, ripped or otherwise past its best. Linen and blankets that aren't suitable for donating can be put in council textile recycling bins, though they don't take old duvets or pillows, which should be put out with the household waste.

Every three to six months

o Take some time at the change of each season to go through your wardrobe and do an audit of what needs mending, altering or dry cleaning. Get rid of anything you think isn't worth the trouble and, if you have room, store out-of-season clothes elsewhere, so they don't crowd out the things you wear every day.

Once a year

o Make a note of anything in your bedroom that needs repairing or replacing. Write down a schedule for it in your decluttering journal (see page 17). Move on any furniture, rugs and other decorative items you no longer love.

CHAPTER SIX

Bathing and laundry

Give yourself a fresh start

What is elegance? Soap and water.

CECIL BEATON

One of the most satisfying aspects of decluttering your home is how much easier it is to keep everything clean – yourself included.

Give your bathroom a break

Bathrooms are among the busiest places in our homes, particularly if we share them with family members or flatmates. They're often the smallest, too, so we invariably demand quite a lot from such cramped spaces. They repay any effort we make to improve them tenfold. A clearer, cleaner bathroom is a much more relaxing place to be and makes it easier to get out of the house in the morning, then do all the 'admin' at night (see page 134).

- Motivate yourself to get started by remembering that clear surfaces are easier to clean, which is particularly important in high-traffic areas such as bathrooms.

- Only keep out on the surfaces things that you use every day. So toothbrushes, toothpaste and shampoo, yes, sunscreen in midwinter, no.

- Pack up extra bottles of shampoo, body wash and other personal hygiene things for which you have duplicates in a box or crate and put them away in a cupboard, out of the bathroom if necessary. Stick a note on top of the box and/or make a record in your decluttering journal (see page 17) of what you've put in there. Before you write your weekly shopping list, check your home stores of soap, shampoo and so on first.

- If you have a small bathroom, take everything off the shelves and place it in a laundry basket in the centre of the room. Give the surfaces, bottles and jars a speedy wipe down, then only put back

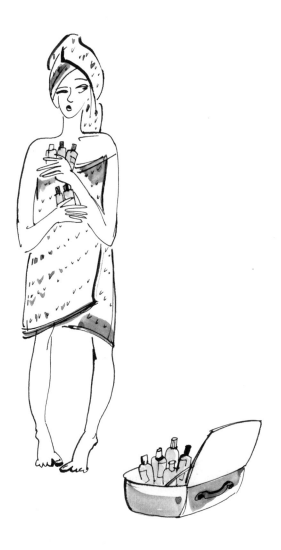

Don't nick toiletries from hotel bathrooms.

the things you use every day. If you have a large bathroom, divide it into zones and work on one zone at a time.

- If you share a bathroom, try to share as many products as possible, too. If you can come to some sort of consensus on toothpaste, mouthwash, shampoo, body wash and soap, such cheering domestic harmony will go a long way to streamlining your bathroom shelves, which can only add to the jollity of the masses.
- In shared bathrooms, if at all possible, each person should have their own drawer or basket. This makes it easier to put things away, which is a hefty part of the decluttering battle.
- Get rid of any unwanted gifts such as lotions and scented candles which aren't to your taste – you're bound to know someone who would love them.
- Don't nick toiletries from hotel bathrooms. The biggest thrill is the act of petty larceny. We seldom use the products afterwards and they only clog up the place. The only justification is if you fly a lot and the dinky bottles are under the liquid allowance. But then, if you fly a lot, you're highly likely to be staying in places with their own dinky bottles of shampoo, and so it continues. Break the cycle.

Make it easy on yourself

Adding some simple storage where you can makes it easier to keep things looking pulled together, and when they're pulled together you're less likely to allow them to get gummed up with extra stuff.

- Install a simple shelf above the door, which is often an unused space. Add a few baskets to store things that you need in the bathroom but not immediately to hand – loo rolls, extra toiletries, cotton wool and so on.

○ I once read a (no doubt apocryphal) story in a magazine that said Martha Stewart didn't own a bathrobe as she went straight from jumping out of bed to being a mogul. No slummocking around for her. For the rest of us, a few hooks on the back of the bathroom door are undoubtedly a good idea.

○ Add a rail or two on which to dry out damp towels. This makes it easy for everyone to keep them tidy and also means they're less likely to grab a fresh one every time they wash their hands, thus creating more lazy laundry (see Wash and wear, page 145). If possible, as you replace your towels, choose a different colour for each member of the household so that everyone knows they're using their own – this might also encourage them to use them more than once.

○ You need a convenient spot for cleaning products. If you don't have a vanity unit, use a crate or box (I keep mine in a small hamper). You don't need much: multipurpose cleaner, limescale remover (see In praise of vinegar and bicarbonate of soda, page 169), loo cleaner and brush and some microfibre cloths will probably do it.

Make-up move along

If you like make-up at all, it's highly likely you own far more than you use. In the search for flawless foundation, you probably bought quite a few before you fixed on the perfect one, and yet the also-rans invariably still clutter up your dressing table because they cost quite a bit, you're reluctant to throw them out and – who knows? – one day the chalky-faced consumptive look may be all the rage and you'll be prepared. Added to that, make-up is a popular impulse buy when we need a bit of a cheer-up. Researchers call it the Lipstick Effect – during difficult times, the sales of lipstick go up as it's an affordable luxury. I tell you what will also cheer you up – not having to wade through all those mistakes to get to what you need and like.

- To help identify the make-up you really use, create a reasonably polished face – the sort of look you might aim for if you're going to an important meeting or a nice lunch. After you use each product, put it into a basket. When you're finished, see what you've got. These are your core products. Allow a few extra things for when you want to go haute glam – a darker lipstick, liquid eyeliner, that sort of thing – then take a very hard look at everything that's left over. You probably don't need any of it at all.

- Make-up has a shelf life. Most dry products such as eyeshadow and powder last a couple of years; 'wet' things, such as foundation, liquid eyeliner or mascara, from six months to a year. When it's past its best, toss it.

- In addition to the above, discard anything that is discoloured, cracked, separated, broken or musty smelling – or tasting, in the case of lipstick or lip balm.

- Throw out any scruffy make-up brushes or sponges – they are terrible breeding grounds for bacteria. To keep brushes in best condition, wash them gently with a tiny dab of shampoo. Rinse them under the tap with the bristles facing downwards, blot dry on a clean facecloth, gently squeezing to remove as much water as possible, then leave them to dry naturally, resting on the facecloth.

Pass it on

If you have sealed, unused toiletries which don't appeal to you, pass them on. Check out @the_beauty_banks on Instagram. It's a non-profit organization which helps to get toiletries and cosmetics into the hands of people living in serious poverty. In the US, beautybus.org donates them to chronically or terminally ill people.

Wash and wear

If we have a significant problem with clutter, our laundry can really get out of hand. What exacerbates this is having too many clothes, which allows us to avoid dealing with our heaps of unwashed and washed laundry until they may as well have their own postcode. We might seize the moment and spend a day doing a lot of loads to deal with the immediate issue, but then we don't factor in enough time to dry everything properly (there are few worse smells than that of sour clothes which have been put away damp; it's pure Eau de Regrette), iron anything that needs ironing, fold things and put them away. Eventually, the dirty stuff gets mixed up with the clean stuff and we're in a worse state than when we started. Then we can't find anything we want to wear, so we go out to buy something new and we intensify the problem rather than solving it. To avoid this:

- o Ruthlessly purge your clothes (see page 126). This may involve sorting through the laundry heap as much as the wardrobe. Keep yourself motivated by reminding yourself that the fewer clothes you have, the less time you'll have to spend laundering them.
- o Look for a double-binned laundry basket which lets you sort your clothes into lights and darks as you go, making things easier.
- o When you next buy a washing machine, look for one that has a quick-wash cycle. Mine has a 14-minute freshening-up wash, which is all a

lot of clothes need if you've only worn them once. It really helps me stay on track if I can do four loads in an hour. A good delicates cycle and wool wash, as well as the ability to manually set the temperature to 20°C or even lower for most cycles, will also cut down on trips to the dry cleaner's, which you are likely to procrastinate yourself out of anyway (see Do not dry clean, opposite).

- If your washer and dryer aren't in the kitchen, make sure you have a bin next to them to dispose of lint from the dryer, rubbish picked from pockets, empty detergent bottles and boxes.

- Toss out broken hangers or anything that might snag your clothes. Sorry to get all Mommie Dearest, but gradually replace wire hangers with ones that are kinder to your clothes. Wooden or padded hangers are great but take up a lot of space on the rail. I like non-slip hangers, which are coated in a sort of Fuzzy-Felt material. They're cheap and can be picked up at most homeware stores and online.

- Get into the habit of folding things straight from the dryer or hanging them on coat hangers to slash the amount of ironing you need to do.

Laundry products

How many products do you really need? Probably fewer than you think.

- A liquid detergent or powder – just find one that suits you. I'm not huge on getting a special one for delicates or woollens, or for hand washing; I just use less of my regular one.

- A fabric conditioner, though you can use distilled white vinegar instead – just add a small cupful to the fabric conditioner dispenser in your machine. It makes your clothes soft, is good for the machine (particularly if you live in a hard-water area) and I promise it doesn't make your clothes smell like a chip shop (see In praise of vinegar and bicarbonate of soda, page 169). Don't add fabric conditioner to washes that contain towels, microfibre cloths and some sportswear as it makes them less absorbent.

o If you have dogs or cats, a biological washing powder is good for removing smells from anything they've wee'd on, as it removes every lingering odour and makes it less likely they will go back to that spot again.

o There are all kinds of specific stain removers, but to be honest I've had just as much luck in most cases by rubbing a bit of neat washing-up liquid on the stain, then leaving for ten minutes or so before I chuck it into the wash.

Do not dry clean

If you're at all inclined to procrastination (hello, you're a living, breathing, decluttering-book-buying person, that's why we're all here), do not buy dry-clean-only clothes. They will sit in a bag in your hallway until you can't remember whether or not that tomato stain is part of the pattern.

But if you lost your head for a moment and bought that dry-clean-only thing, all is not lost. Yes, Cinderella, you may wear it more than once in a millennium. Because the truth is, most clothes with that procrastinator-unfriendly label on them can quite easily be washed at home – it's just clothes manufacturers covering themselves because they don't trust us to clean our own stuff properly.

Of course, don't put your cashmere coat on a hot wash, but most cotton, linen, polyester and woollen knits can be gently hand-washed or put through a cool delicates wash in your machine. Test an inconspicuous area for colour fastness first by dipping the corner of a clean, white cloth in diluted detergent and rubbing it against the fabric. To protect your clothes further, turn them inside out and put them into a mesh bag or pillowcase before putting them into the machine. Dry knits by spreading them out on a flat surface; put other pieces on coat hangers to drip dry.

Out, damn moths

Modern houses that are warm and well insulated, mild winters, and the increase in popularity of vintage clothes and furnishings have led to a massive boom in the clothes-moth population – English Heritage reports this has more than doubled in five years. If you have a cluttered house, you're more susceptible to moths because they thrive in dark, crammed, unaired wardrobes and drawers. They are particularly drawn to dirty clothes and find sweat, body oils and food spills ambrosial. Don't say I didn't warn you.

When people tell me to tuck a few lavender bags or cedar balls about the place, it's all I can do not to laugh in their faces. This might make moths marginally less likely to visit you on their holidays, but it will do precisely nothing if you have an infestation of these creatures made from dust and hatred. This is what you need to do:

- Keep a very close eye out for their webs or cocoons and act immediately. Don't delay for a second.
- Wash everything that can be washed at over 60°C immediately. Anything that wouldn't survive such a hot wash, such as sweaters or silks, seal in plastic bags and put them in the freezer for a week, which should kill the larvae.

○ Vacuum everything and discard the bag outside the house, or empty the cylinder into a bag outside the house.

○ Wash down surfaces.

○ I am mad keen on the Moth Stop products sold by Lakeland (lakeland.co.uk) and the sticky pheromone traps that work by luring the male moths to their deaths before they can fertilize any eggs. Check out the pleasingly named mothkiller.co.uk for these.

○ Stay vigilant.

Let go of perfect

One of my mother's favourite sayings, along with, 'Good enough is good enough', is the great G. K. Chesterton quotation, 'If a thing is worth doing, it is worth doing badly.' This is not an invitation to put in a poor shift; quite the opposite, in fact. It's about putting your heart into something and not worrying too much about being flawless. It's about making mistakes, building on past errors and just keeping going.

In this decluttering process, of course it's tempting if you have the funds just to get someone else in to do all the hard work for you, and there are certainly times when some of us might need a bit of support (see When to get help, page 54). But don't think anyone can do this job for you better than you can do it for yourself. You are creating your own perfectly imperfect bespoke system, and though you might need a hand sometimes, with every small job you tackle you are building new skills and transforming your home from a source of dissatisfaction and stress into a place that truly nurtures you.

Quick bathroom and laundry fixes

If you have five minutes

○ Go through your clothes and pick out anything that needs dry cleaning. Decide if it really does need dry cleaning (see Do not dry clean, page 147).

○ Throw out old bottles and sprays of sunscreen. If it doesn't have an expiry date stamped on it, ditch anything that's more than a year old or has a musty smell.

○ Chuck out old make-up. It can be a smorgasbord of bacteria.

If you have ten minutes

○ Take everything off a bathroom shelf. Only put back what you use every day, or at least every week. Put the rest away.

○ Go through your bathroom cleaning products. Be ruthless about throwing away anything you don't use.

If you have thirty minutes

○ Do some hand washing.

○ Start tackling Laundry Mountain if it's got a bit out of hand.

Calendar

Once a week

○ Before you write your weekly shopping list, check your home stores of soap, shampoo and so on.

Once a month

○ Check any gadgets such as shavers, electric toothbrushes, hair dryers and straighteners. Discard any you no longer use.

Every three to six months

○ Check the expiry dates on medications and take anything old or no longer needed to your local pharmacy for disposal.

○ Ditch any cleaning products you don't use.

○ Have a look through your towels. Any that are a bit too tatty for human use can be donated to your local animal shelter.

Once a year

○ Make a note of anything in your bedroom that needs repairing or replacing. Write down a schedule for that in your decluttering journal (see page 17). Discard any furniture, rugs and decorative items you no longer love.

CHAPTER SEVEN

Around the edges

Procrastination central

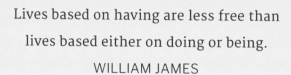

Lives based on having are less free than
lives based either on doing or being.

WILLIAM JAMES

Around the edges of our homes are those areas perhaps most prone to becoming dumping grounds. Few of us use them every day, so it's remarkably easy to fill them with things we don't have proper homes for and forget about them – that is until we desperately need something we buried underneath layers and layers of procrastination. Don't let another summer go by without using your deck chairs or barbecue because you'd have to excavate the shed to get to them, or attempt to survive another winter without your big coat and boots because you've forgotten where you put them in in the attic.

It's time to tackle the don't-make-me-go-in-there challenges of sheds and garages, cellars and attics, and those mobile procrastination units, cars. You're up to this. We've come so far together, there's nothing we can't face.

Cellars and attics

Cellars are slightly more prone to becoming dumping grounds than attics, as attics are usually less accessible. Personally, I am saved by the entrance to our attic being about the size of a biscuit tin, so it's almost impossible to get anything up there. But essentially the principles are the same. Both can become the final resting places – or near final resting places, as you're about to tackle them – of bits of wood which aren't quite large enough to do anything with, orphaned lids and jars, equipment from activities and sports you no longer pursue (but you keep them in case you revive your passion for Nordic walking, basket weaving or spoon whittling), bikes the kids have outgrown, tins and tins of old paint, unwanted gifts, half-finished DIY projects and broken furniture you think you're going to get around to mending one day (no, you're laughing).

- As a priority – do this before you do anything else – clear the top of the cellar steps. Squeezing past all manner of junk just to get to the staircase is like the beginning of an episode of *Casualty*. Make sure you can get in and out of cellars and attics safely, especially as you will probably be carrying bulky objects back and forth.

- It's very tempting to think that in order to sort out these areas, you have to remove everything before you start. In an ideal world that would be great, but that's why many of us never get around to tackling these spaces – ideal conditions never present themselves. Approach this a bit at a time. Better to do 20 minutes of decluttering every evening for a week than to promise yourself you will set aside a whole weekend to tackle it and then never getting around to it because, you know, life.

- Be realistic about what you're going to keep. Just because five years ago, you fancied yourself as an upcycler of junk-shop furniture, it doesn't matter that your interests and tastes have now changed. Forgive yourself for those incomplete projects and get them out of the house.

- Do you really need all your dad's old tools if the closest you ever get to DIY is changing a lightbulb? Let them go.

- Sort through your leftover paint and only keep what you might need to use for touch-ups of your present colour scheme. We dispose of 50 million litres of paint in the UK each year, which is terribly wasteful, particularly as it is hard to recycle. Consider donating paint to communityrepaint.org.uk, which redistributes leftover paint to community groups and people in social need.

Anything you can't donate, harden off by stirring in sand or sawdust and leaving it to dry out before dropping it off at your nearest household waste recycling centre (they won't accept it while it is still liquid and for about 800 reasons you really mustn't just pour it down the sink). In the US, paintcare.org donates and recycles unwanted paint.

Sheds and garages

These are just the fresh-air versions of cellars and attics and, like cellars and attics, we frequently put off tackling them until we think we have time to sort them out in one go. This can be a challenge, as it's often dependent on having a spot of fine weather to shift everything outside, but then when the sun's out there are a million things most of us would rather do than heave heavy, often grubby, things about. The only way to get through it is to see every bit of your dejunking efforts as an investment in future sunny days, when you will be able to sit on your good garden furniture while something delicious grills on the barbecue without having to half kill yourself to retrieve them from their storage space before you get started.

- o Go through any out-of-date or broken gardening equipment with a ruthless eye. I kept a lovely, sharp lawn-edger for years after we no longer had a lawn because it was such a beautifully made thing and my dad had given it to me.
- o Discard any old, musty bags of bird feed.
- o Either repair or get rid of any garden furniture that is broken or otherwise past its best.
- o Ditch any kitschy garden stuff you've been given as gifts, unless it's to your taste, of course (and that's obviously *fine*). I am thinking

particularly of those invitations to robbery, the signs you're supposed to hang on the front door that say things like, 'We're in the garden'.

- Go through your ceramic and terracotta plant pots and discard any that are cracked, broken or otherwise wouldn't make it through another winter. Keep just enough broken crocks as you might need to add drainage to other pots.
- Make a pile of plastic plant-carrying trays and plastic plant pots; unless you grow a lot from seed you really don't need to keep them. Check with local garden centres if they will accept them for recycling.
- Throw out any broken brooms, mops or other bits of shonky cleaning equipment that have been cast out from the bosom of the home into the cold embrace of the garage or shed.

Clean car drill

Don't allow your car to become a mobile dumping ground or storage unit or, worse, a filing cabinet of filth. In our pre-decluttered days, my husband used to keep his golf clubs in the car boot, even though he played approximately twice a year, simply because we didn't have room for them in the house. This made me hate golf even more than the entirely rational amount.

- Keep a roll of small bin liners – the kind you might buy by accident and then get them home to find they're pedal-bin sized. This time, buy them on purpose and keep them to hand in the glove compartment for when you need to declutter your car after a long journey.

The only way to get through it is to see every bit of your dejunking
efforts as an investment in future sunny days.

- Imagine you're picking your mum up from the station in an hour. That should motivate you to get rid of all the banana skins and fast-food containers.
- Keep some bags in the boot, all of them stored inside the biggest one, but only as many as you need for your average, regular grocery shop.
- Encourage children – even small ones – to take their stuff with them each time they get out of the car, including rubbish.
- Put jump leads, oil, de-icer and a scraper and anything else you require for a basic car-maintenance kit into a small crate in the boot so it all stays neatly together and you can lay your hands on it when you need it.

Quick fixes for the outer edges

🕐 If you have five minutes
- Scoop up any plastic plant pots and enquire at the local garden centre if they can recycle them.

🕐 If you have ten minutes
- Clear the inevitable coffee-cup zone (see page 27) that is the top of the cellar steps.

◑ **If you have thirty minutes**

○ Discard any abandoned DIY jobs or craft projects. Break them down into their component parts if you must, but even better, just get them out.

Calendar

Once a week

○ Make sure entrances to cellars and attics are clear.

Once a month

○ Have a quick sweep around your car if you have one and remove anything that doesn't need to be in there.

Every three to six months

○ Arrange to give any bikes, sporting equipment and other large toys your children no longer use to someone who will really enjoy them. There are an increasing number of social enterprises throughout the country that will be delighted to take your old bikes off your hands; Google for one near you.

- Get rid of any garden furniture that is beyond repair.
- Get rid of any paint tins that are surplus to requirements (see page 154).

Once a year

- Go through your Christmas decorations, ideally in January as you are putting them away, and discard any that are broken or that you no longer care for.
- Take stock of any electric-, gas- or diesel-powered gardening equipment. Dispose of anything broken or that you no longer use.

CHAPTER EIGHT

Keeping it clean

Done and dusted

Nothing diminishes anxiety faster
than action.
WALTER ANDERSON

Decluttering and cleaning often go hand in hand, if only because during the course of decluttering we begin to see surfaces we might not have laid eyes on for years. It also becomes so much easier to clean up when we're not faced with the daily domestic steeplechase of too much stuff. It's less of a chore and becomes infinitely more rewarding, as we really begin to see our homes take shape, into ones that reflect our tastes, where we feel relaxed and happy and entirely at home.

It's often said that cleaning your house is like polishing yourself. I think that this is a golden rule. It isn't just dust and dirt that accumulate in our homes. It's also the shadows of our past selves that let that dust and dirt continue to build. Cleaning the grime is certainly unpleasant, but more than that, it's the need to face our own past deeds that makes it so tough. But when we have fewer material possessions and cleaning becomes an easy habit, the shadows we now face will be of our daily accomplishments. FUMIO SASAKI

Worst thing, first thing

One of the habits we develop and strengthen through the decluttering process is that of working out what our intentions are at each stage, setting our priorities and not putting things off because we're afraid of not doing them perfectly. If you start with what you think will be the most difficult task – the one you've been avoiding – it usually isn't as difficult or time consuming as you think. Crossing it off will give you a tremendous boost. In your decluttering journal (see page 17), schedule a time to tackle a Task of Doom for each area of your home. Do one today. Breathe out.

You do not get gold stars for cleaning your toilet. In actual life, there is a depressing lack of stickers.
ALEXANDRA PETRI

Tidy like a housekeeper

These women – it's almost always women – know what they're doing and don't mess around, particularly hotel housekeepers who may have dozens of rooms to sort out in a day. They have a system which means they can work methodically without having to waste time overthinking things. It becomes automatic.

o First, open the window to air the room.

o Next, remove any obvious clutter. Empty wastepaper baskets, bin any rubbish and place anything that needs to go into another room by the door.

o Now, starting at the door, proceed clockwise around the room, working high to low, so that you're not sending any dust cascading down onto things you've already cleaned.

o Vacuum or sweep, then mop.

o Stack books, fold or hang clothes, fold throws, plump pillows and cushions, make bed/s.

Things to do while you're doing something else

I know I talk about not multitasking (see page 35), and I do firmly believe that, in order to achieve the best results, focus is very important. Do what you're doing, remember? But this is just letting time do some of the hard work for you.

o Descale the kettle. Unplug it and quarter-fill it with distilled white vinegar, then leave it for an hour. Empty it, give the inside a gentle scrub with a scrubby sponge, then rinse well with clean water. Fill to the maximum water level with clean water from the tap, bring to the boil, discard the water and the kettle is ready to use. (For more miraculous things to do with vinegar, see page 169.)

○ Clean the microwave. Pour a cupful of water into a microwavable bowl, cut a lemon in half and squeeze in the juice, then toss the halves into the bowl. Heat the water on high for three minutes, then leave for five to ten minutes without opening the door so the steam can do its work, softening grubby splashes and grease. Open the microwave, remove the turntable and either wash it in the sink or pop it in the dishwasher. Take a microfibre cloth soaked in hot water and wrung out tightly, and wipe down the inside of the microwave; leave the door open so it can dry and air out before putting the turntable back in place.

Tea-break whip around

I work from home, so I often use going downstairs from my office to make a cup of tea as a punctuation point in the day. It helps me to gather my thoughts before I move on to the next thing. (You might call this procrastination, but that would be unkind.)

To tie in with my philosophy that every small thing you do moves you towards your goal, I use the three minutes it takes me to boil the kettle to undertake a few micro-organizing and cleaning tasks which help to keep me on top of things. This isn't the time for a deep declutter and clean – it's simply doing what you can in the time you have.

○ Load or unload the dishwasher
○ Sweep the floor
○ Mop the floor
○ Put a wash on or fold some laundry
○ Go through a heap of mail

- Take the rubbish out
- Sort the recycling
- Tidy up and put away some coats and shoes from the hallway
- Open a window. Our grandmothers understood the importance of keeping a house ventilated, but in this world of centrally heated, double-glazed, well-insulated homes it's something we often forget. Try to throw open the windows in every room you use for at least a few minutes a day
- Wipe down the top of the cooker
- Tidy a shelf or drawer in the fridge or freezer
- Wipe down the handles of the fridge. An environmental health inspector once told me these were often the most germ-laden part of any kitchen: people are touching them a hundred times a day, which makes them ripe for cross-contamination
- Wipe down the counter tops
- Tidy a drawer or shelf
- Meditate. I'm not kidding. Micro-meditating is sometimes all that stands between me and passive-aggressive tutting (see page 123)

Whatever gets you through

Very few people love to clean; at least I'm guessing very few people who might consider buying this book love to clean. This is what I know: we all need to build in rewards wherever we can. Whatever it takes. Remember I told you about my fantasy life where I live in France for half of the year (see page 72)? Yes, about that. An indulgence I give myself is to buy cleaning products, laundry detergent and fabric conditioner from French Click (frenchclick.co.uk), a mail-order company that sells French groceries, toiletries and cleaning materials. This means my freshly laundered sheets smell like holidays, which I would say is quite the incentive to change the bedlinen. I also buy from them a multipurpose cleaner, St Marc au Savon Noir et Fleur d'Oranger, because I love its orange-blossom smell. I have a friend who is a devout Catholic and who loves a fabric conditioner that smells like incense (Comfort Perfume Deluxe Lavish Blossom, if you're wondering). Find something, anything, that makes it easier for you to get down to it. Build in secret rewards to make chores more appealing. I won't tell anyone.

Clean-up kit

We spoke earlier about the under-the-sink cupboard (see page 81) which is often crammed with things you don't need. I get it. I've done it. You buy the special sticky-label remover (use cheap veg oil), limescale buster (use distilled white vinegar) and scouring cream (bicarbonate of soda is your friend) because you think if you've bought the product, you've done the job. Not true. Get rid of all those mysterious, long-forgotten tubs and sprays and gather together your new, low-maintenance kit:

Cleaning becomes less of a chore and becomes infinitely more rewarding, as we really begin to see our homes take shape.

- Scrubby sponges and non-scratch scourers
- Multipurpose spray
- Washing-up liquid
- Microfibre cloths
- Cloths roughly cut up from old, lint-free sheets or T-shirts. And/or paper towels
- A few old toothbrushes to get into nooks and crannies
- Distilled white vinegar (see page 169)
- Bicarbonate of soda (see page 169)
- Loo cleaner
- Floor cleaner
- Wood cleaner or waxes; I like Bald's Wood Furniture Balm and Town Talk Lavender Furniture Wax
- Metal polish for silver, brass and copper, if you have things made out of those materials
- A mildly abrasive, non-scratch cleaner for when the bicarb won't quite cut it; I like Bar Keepers Friend Power Cream

TIPS

• Mix bicarb with neat washing-up liquid to make a quick, gentle scouring cream.

• Sprinkle bicarb on rugs and leave for a few hours or overnight before vacuuming, to freshen and remove any smells. This is a kinder, gentler Shake n'Vac (it really does put the freshness back).

In praise of vinegar and bicarbonate of soda

Distilled white vinegar and bicarbonate of soda are so cheap and are brilliant for all kinds of household cleaning.

- Dilute one part water to one part vinegar in a spray bottle and you can use it for pretty much anything. Drip in a couple of drops of essential oils (lavender, any citrus oil) if the smell bothers you, but the aroma of Eau de Chip Shop dissipates fairly quickly. Use it to clean sinks, greasy counters and stove tops and to clean up oven spills.

- Pour a cupful of vinegar into a blender, whizz up and leave for five minutes before rinsing and drying to remove any lingering odours.

- I throw a cupful of vinegar in the bottom of my dishwasher each week and run it, empty, on the quick rinse cycle to keep it clean.

- For especially dirty pans, chuck in a handful of bicarb and a good slosh of vinegar and leave for 30 minutes – it will fizz up in a pleasingly dramatic fashion, giving you the feeling something is really happening. Give it a good rub down with a scrubby sponge and repeat if necessary.

- Sprinkle a cupful of bicarb down the plughole in the sink, followed by a cup of vinegar. Leave for 20–30 minutes, then pour down a kettleful of boiling water to eliminate any bad smells and help alleviate any small blockages. In fact, if I've been washing up particularly greasy pans and dishes, I often just tip a kettle of boiling water down the plughole afterwards in an effort to move any grease on its way.

Afterword

Home is the nicest word there is.

LAURA INGALLS WILDER

There. That's it. I've shared with you my maximalist's guide to, well, not quite minimalism, but to creating your own, uniquely sustainable method of dragging calm from the greedy jaws of chaos. I hope you are less overwhelmed by your stuff, and that you now know a home where you feel happy and nurtured is absolutely within your grasp, even if you're not quite there yet.

Decluttering can sometimes feel challenging, but as long as you keep on doing the next thing, as long as you keep on sorting, tossing and donating, you will create a more tranquil life for yourself. You cannot fail. The absolute minimum you will achieve is a life less encumbered by your possessions, but I feel I should warn you here, before it's too late, that sometimes the effects of these changes can be quite dramatic. If a life full of clutter has been dragging you down, hemming you in, draining your energy, well – look out world! – here you come. Decluttering can create a slightly euphoric feeling, a feeling that if you can tackle this, you can tackle anything. Not only will you have more time, you will have more energy, more confidence, more physical and emotional space, to live more boldly and less apologetically.

So off you go, stride into your life, knowing that if you fall back a little, you can start again right where you are, and that you will be fine. You've absolutely got this.

Do what you have to do until

you can do what you want to do.

OPRAH WINFREY

Other things to read

I've deliberately kept this quite short because, well, you know. Uncluttered.

- Rachel Hoffman, *Unf*ck Your Habitat: You're Better Than Your Mess (Bluebird, 2016)*

- Karen Kingston, *Creating Sacred Space with Feng Shui (Piatkus, 1996)*

- Marie Kondo, *The Life-Changing Magic of Tidying: A Simple, Effective Way to Banish Clutter Forever (Vermilion, 2014)*

- Marie Kondo, *Spark Joy: An Illustrated Guide to the Japanese Art of Tidying (Vermilion, 2017)*

- David J. Linden, *The Compass of Pleasure: How Our Brains Make Fatty Foods, Orgasm, Exercise, Marijuana, Generosity, Vodka, Learning, and Gambling Feel So Good (Penguin Books, 2012)*

- Dominique Loreau, *L'Art de la Simplicité: How to Live More with Less (Orion Books, 2016, English edition)*

- Margareta Magnusson, *The Gentle Art of Swedish Death Cleaning: How to Free Yourself and Your Family From A Lifetime of Clutter (Canongate Books, 2017)*

- Cheryl Mendelson, *Home Comforts: The Art and Science of Keeping House (Scribner Book Company, 2005)*

- Julie Morgenstern, *Organizing from the Inside Out: The Foolproof System for Organizing Your Home, Your Office, and Your Life* (Henry Holt, 1998)

- Fumio Sasaki, *Goodbye, Things: On Minimalist Living* (Penguin Books, 2015)

- Deniece Schofield, *Confessions of an Organized Homemaker: The Secrets of Uncluttering Your Home and Taking Control of Your Life* (Betterway Books, 1994)

- *Martha Stewart's Homekeeping Handbook: The Essential Guide to Caring for Everything in Your Home* (Clarkson Potter, 2006)

- James Wallman, *Stuffocation: Living More with Less* (Penguin Books, 2015)

Online resources

- Buddhify.com

- Calm.com

- Flylady.net

- Linda Hall's audiomeditation.co.uk

- Headspace.com

- Theminimalists.com

Index

5 Fling 122
10 Commandments 60–1
15 Fling 66
30-day challenge 56–7, 107, 123

A
appliances 71–2, 116, 151
attics 153–5, 159

B
bags 128–30, 136
bathrooms 139–44, 150
bedrooms 118–38
beds 119–120, 137
bicarbonate of soda 168, 169
books 30, 73, 89, 97, 106–7, 115

C
cars 156, 158, 159
CDs 98
cellars 153–5, 158, 159
charity shops 39–40, 129
Christmas stuff 75, 160
cleaning 54–5, 161–9
  products 81, 143, 150, 151, 166, 168

clothes 118, 126–9, 138
  laundry 123, 145–7, 150
  passing on 128, 131, 136
coffee cup zones 20, 27–8, 78
companions, declutter 132–3
cookware 80
crockery 75–7, 81

D
desks 102, 104, 115
digital storage 73, 110, 112
dining rooms 75
domestic harmony 52–3
drawers 105
drinks 80–1
dry cleaning 147–9

E
electrical cables 105
email 110, 112
emotional attachment 16, 29–32, 108
Evening 15 61, 86, 134–5

F
feng shui 20–1, 132

flatmates 53–5
Flylady 30, 66
food 74, 80–81
freecycle 56
freezers 79–80

G
garages 155–6
garden equipment 155–6, 160
glasses 131

H
hallways 83, 90–91
herbs and spices 69–71, 81
home offices 101–119
housekeepers, tidying like 163

I
inherited items 58–9, 108

J
journals 16–18, 19, 28, 34, 64–5, 86, 108, 118, 128
'just in case' items 45–6, 72

K
kettles 163
khouneh tekouni 24

kids: artwork 108–9, 115
   bedrooms 120–3
   toys 91–4, 97
kitchens 62–81

L

landings 83
laundry 136, 137, 145–50
letting things go 11, 39, 72, 132
lists 17–19, 35, 110
living areas 82–99

M

make-up 143–4, 150
medication 151
meditation 32, 123–5
microwaves 164
moths 148–9
motivation 113–15
mugs 79

N

newspapers 20, 75, 97, 115
nurturing your house 59

O

oils/condiments 78–9

P

paint 153–5, 160
paperwork 101–116
parties 55

perfectionism 61, 149
personal items 107–9
pets 91, 94–96, 132, 147
photographs 97
plant pots 156, 158
plants 96
plastic containers 73–4, 80
procrastination 36, 40, 43, 128, 147

R

recipes 73
recycling bins 77, 87
repurposing items 108
rewards 20, 25, 41, 61

S

self-storage 38
self-worth 30
selling items 40–1, 87, 98
shaking the house 23–4
shared living 48–55
sheds 155–6
shoes and boots 127, 136
shopping 41, 43, 77
shredders 104
sinks 66, 68
skinny fat homes 46–8
social media 115
stairs 83, 90–91
storage 60, 87, 134
   bathroom 142–3

digital 110, 112
hallway 88
paperwork 113
work areas 102
surfaces, kitchen 68–9
Swedish death cleaning 22–3, 108

T

tea-break whip arounds 164–5
tea towels 78
technology 105
timescale 29, 61
toiletries 140–4, 150–1
towels 143, 151
toys 91–4, 97, 99

V

vinegar 169
virtual clutter 110, 115–6

W

wallets/purses 128–30, 136
wastepaper baskets 87
work areas 101–115

Acknowledgements

Writing this book would not have been nearly as much fun without the whole team of people who helped me along. At Kyle Books, I am enormously grateful to Kyle Cathie, who first approached me about this project, and also to Joanna Copestick who steered it along. Thanks too, to editor Tara O'Sullivan for her enthusiasm from the very first, for putting up with me, and for making the whole process such a pleasure, and to editorial assistant, Sarah Kyle, and production manager, Lisa Pinnell for working so hard on my behalf. I am grateful for the eagle eye of copy editor, Caroline Taggart, and for designer Cathy McKinnon's cool, clear style. Massive thanks to illustrator, Alyana Cazalet, whose warm, funny illustrations capture perfectly the tone I wanted for this book.

Thank you to Caroline Michel and Tessa David at Peters, Fraser and Dunlop for excellent agenting, and to my friends Jack Monroe and Julia Platt Leonard for allowing me to share their decluttering thoughts. Much love to Victoria Harper always, for the help, advice, and mostly for making me laugh for twenty-five years.

On the home team, I am indebted to Darina Nyagolova for all of her hard work and cheerfulness in keeping this show on the road, and to Virginia Hiller, who has taught me so much.

And most of all, thank you Séan Donnellan, for absolutely everything.